SKI
INC. .

My journey through four decades
in the ski-resort business,
from the founding entrepreneurs
to mega-companies.

PRAISE FOR

Ski Inc.

"Chris Diamond arrived in Steamboat Springs in the late 1990s as president
of the Steamboat Ski & Resort Corporation. From the beginning, he faced
resentment and hostility from residents of the town who detested the
presence of the American Skiing Company, the new owners of the resort
and Chris' employers. In part, this is the story of how, over the next 17
years, with skill and grit and determination, he led the company through
tumultuous times to a restored place of prominence in the industry.
He also became one of the most respected and admired residents of this
little town in northwestern Colorado."

VERNE LUNDQUIST
CBS Sports

"A true ski-resort pioneer and legend, Chris Diamond presents an
entertaining and educational behind-the-scenes picture of the romantic,
rough-and-tumble ski-resort business. A must-read for anyone who
wonders if there is money to be made in the business."

STEVE REINEMUND
Retired Chairman and CEO, PepsiCo
Former Dean of Business, Wake Forest University

"In the ski industry, Chris Diamond was always one the smartest guys in the
room, and now we learn that he is also a talented storyteller. This is a page-
turner for anyone who works in skiing—or has a passion for the sport. It's
an opportunity to relive or learn the behind-the-scene details of resort
leadership, from everyday operations to the seminal moments in our
history."

MICHAEL BERRY
President, National Ski Areas Association

"For nearly a half-century, Chris Diamond made countless contributions to the ski industry, including shaping mountain resorts and trade associations. *Ski Inc.* offers his unique perspective on the evolution of ski areas from small, hands-on operations to big business. It also sheds light on the many interesting characters who have left indelible marks on our industry—and who made the sport what it is today."

ROB PERLMAN
President and Chief Operating Officer, Steamboat Ski & Resort Corporation

"This book is rich in history and business. Chris' background and experience rip back the curtain on a few of our classic characters. At its core, the book captures his love of the sport—and the unique personalities we are blessed to share it with."

JERRY BLANN
President, Jackson Hole Mountain Resort

"Anyone who is passionate about skiing and ski towns will gain new insights from *Ski Inc.* Chris is uniquely situated through his four-decade career in ski-area management to recognize the mistakes made and triumphs celebrated as North American resorts matured. He shows a willingness to point out missteps taken along the way. Yet, it isn't in his makeup to trash anyone. And he's as inclined to praise his toughest competitors as he is his own mentors."

TOM ROSS
Staff Writer, *Steamboat Pilot* and *Today*

"An incredibly insightful and comprehensive personal recollection of 40-plus years of the ski industry—and its key resorts, personalities, and organizations—by someone who lived it. Very well written—and a worthwhile read even for those who are not involved in skiing."

FOSTER T. CHANDLER
Former Marketing Director, Killington and S-K-I Ltd.

STEAMBOAT RESORT/© LARRY PIERCE PHOTO

SKI
INC.

My journey through four decades
in the ski-resort business,
from the founding entrepreneurs
to mega-companies.

CHRIS DIAMOND

Edited by Andy Bigford

SKI DIAMOND PUBLISHING
Steamboat Springs, Colorado

Published by Ski Diamond Publishing
P.O. Box 774763, Steamboat Springs, CO 80477
Contact the author at cdiamond1968@gmail.com

Book design by Boulder Bookworks, Boulder, Colorado

Proofreading by Kellee Katagi

Cover, back-cover background and inside-back-cover photos:
Steamboat Resort /© Larry Pierce Photos

First Edition

ISBN 978-0-9979784-0-7

Library of Congress Control Number: 2016913722

Printed in Canada

20 19 18 17   02 03 04 05 06 07

For all the skiers and riders
who buy lift tickets or season passes,
and make it possible for someone like me
to live the dream.

And to all my colleagues,
especially at Killington, Mount Snow, and Steamboat,
who made this journey
a great learning experience
and, yes, so much fun.

CONTENTS

ACKNOWLEDGMENTS

My mother, Mary Diamond, who just turned 95 years old, and my sister, Barbara, still live in our family home at 21 Park Street in Easthampton, Massachusetts. Over the years, they surely have wondered when I was going to grow up and get a real job. But they never said that. Thanks to both of you for letting me chase my dream, for always being there, and for helping make all this possible.

My wife, Eileen, and our grown children, Keenen and Elizabeth, were always in the boat with me helping to row, and not bashful about suggesting a change of direction from time to time. With you guys, running a ski resort was a family affair. You were on every team, though never on the payroll. Thanks for your patience and support, even when we had to move in and out of four houses in five years. This book simply would not have happened without each of you.

To Foster Chandler and Pres Smith. My career had to begin somewhere, and I'm thankful it began with the two of you. Thanks for taking a chance on me, for defining what "exceptional" really means, and for your lifelong friendship.

To my graduate school professor, Dr. John Teunissen, who rekindled my love of reading and is largely responsible for my ability to do that well. Keep sending me updated reading lists, and yes, I will try a more serious writing project sometime...

And as to the writing, thanks to my editor, Andy Bigford. Andy and I had parallel careers in the ski business, he on the media side and myself in operations. His insight from the "other side" was invaluable as we put this writing project together. Andy, your light touch is everywhere. You were a pleasure to work with ... and we even made our deadline.

Chris Diamond
Steamboat Springs, Colorado
September 1, 2016

INTRODUCTION

On June 30, 2015, I retired from my position as the president and chief operating officer of the Steamboat Ski & Resort Corporation, bringing an almost 45-year career in the ski business to a close.

For those of you who already made the move, it's no surprise to learn that the No. 1 question we get from friends and cohorts is, "Well, what are you going to do now?"

My short answer was, and still is: "Not worry about the weather, read more, bike more, ski more . . . and write a book."

There have been many books written on skiing and ski history, including personal stories, such as Dick Durrance's *The Man on the Medal*, and biographies of competitors ranging from the Mahres to Picabo Street and Bode Miller. A must-read for anyone focused on history is John Fry's *The Story of Modern Skiing*. And there has always been a small market for the critical tomes, think *Downhill Slide* by Hal Clifford or Porter Fox's *DEEP: The Story of Skiing and the Future of Snow*.

But to my knowledge, no one has presented a "view from the inside," an exploration of what it's been like to be a part of this industry for 40-plus years as a resort chief at many of its critical moments. My advantage as a storyteller is twofold: the companies I worked for were central to the dynamic evolution of the business over four decades; and secondly, I was deeply involved with governance at the state and national level, witnessing change from that perspective as well. I thought an "insider's history" would be of interest to anyone who was part of the story, as well as anyone with a genuine curiosity about the ski business—where it's been and where it might be going.

I did not grow up, as my children did, in a ski town. At various times, Keenen and Elizabeth enjoyed the Mount Snow Academy, the Killington Mountain School, and the Steamboat Springs Winter Sports Club. (Need I mention they are exceptional skiers?)

My start was more appropriate to the 1950s. I grew up in Easthampton,

Massachusetts, a small factory town close to the academic centers of Northampton and Amherst. My mother had skied in college at Smith, and her old wooden skis were stored in the basement. While I don't remember her actually skiing with my sister, Barbara, and me, I can remember both my mother and father making the drive to Berkshire Snow Basin in our black '54 Chevy. They watched.

My Aunt Jacqueline was the more committed skier, and soon she took over responsibility to get us kids, including my cousin Allen Devine, to Snow Basin, our closest hill. We worked for our free pass by boot-packing the one main rope-tow-serviced slope. At 14 years old, it was more fun than work. We then advanced to the "new" Mount Tom ski area, just over the mountain from East-hampton, literally a 10-minute drive. Mount Tom was managed by Cal Con-niff, who would become the president of the National Ski Areas Association (NSAA) and a longtime friend. Who would have thought? I have wonderful memories of Friday night skiing with other teenagers, always complaining about how expensive the hot chocolate was. Well, some things don't change. I never took a ski lesson that I can remember, certainly not "racing" lessons. But I had the bug. I had no idea that I would ever make a career out of skiing. It would have been almost too much to dream for.

I HAD A PRETTY CLEAR IDEA OF THE KEY STORY LINES when I sat down to write. It was deciding where to start that was difficult. I began continuous, full-time employment in the ski-resort business in October of 1972, just a few months after my discharge from the U.S. Army and safe return from the Re-public of Vietnam. I worried that many of my readers were not even born then, so perhaps it wouldn't be a relevant starting point . . . a time before PCs, smartphones . . . think rotary-dial phones.

Starting in 1972 would lend continuity to the story. I was, from that point on, totally immersed in the ski business, without distraction or material time off, for an entire working career. I was also able to experience the growth of the industry though numerous resort-management positions and different ownership groups. I had the opportunity to witness the evolution of the busi-ness from several geographical perspectives as well, from New England to the Colorado Rockies and even Southern California. Beginning then also allowed me to track the transition from entrepreneurial, single-resort ownership to the now ubiquitous multiresort, public-company structure.

What follows are loosely connected stories of what were, in retrospect, seminal moments in the ski industry, from my early Killington years, to the American Skiing Company's rapid rise and fall, and finally to Steamboat's experience with multiple ownerships.

I also offer my thoughts on where the ski industry has been and where it might be going. I hope one takeaway will be an appreciation of how dramatically the business of skiing has changed over the past four decades, but also how certain basic themes reoccur. I do weave in the story of how our NSAA merged with and then divorced from Ski Industries of America (SIA), as it speaks to the confounding nature of ski operators.

I apologize in advance for errors of memory. Please trust that I have made my best efforts to reconstruct these events. I have no motivation to alter the facts, and the stories, frankly, need no embellishment. This is testimony to the many incredible characters you will meet in the following pages: not your normal 9-to-5 crowd.

"Is it true that you get to ski all the time?" That was one of my "most frequently asked questions." Stick with me through the following chapters, and I hope you'll have a good sense of what it's really like.

As an old friend often remarked, "You can't make this stuff up." I hope you agree. Enjoy.

CHAPTER 1

Welcome to the Ski Business:

Killington in the Late 1970s

O n October 20, 1972, I started my job as assistant to the president at Killington Ski Area. The actual name of the company that owned the resort was Sherburne Corporation. Its founder and president was Preston Leete Smith, a lanky, crew-cut blond, with unbound energy and passion for skiing. On that October day, I really had no idea that skiing would become my vocation as well as avocation.

I had recently mustered out of the Army and was not thinking clearly about what the future held. I considered going back to graduate school (having completed course work for a master's degree in the Graduate School of English at the University of Massachusetts, Amherst, prior to my military service). By the fall of 1972, virtually all of my classmates had moved on with completed PhDs to teaching jobs.

My advisor and good friend, Dr. John Teunissen, had left Amherst for the Department Chair position at the University of Manitoba. Returning to Amherst didn't resonate. I visited John in September and briefly considered Manitoba, but I wasn't ready to make that commitment. While it was early September, temperatures barely broke above freezing, and I noted something unusual about the vehicles. All had a plug protruding from the front grill. This was, as I learned, so block heaters could be plugged in each night, ensuring the car would start in the morning. Winnipeg is, indeed, a cold place in the winter. So I looked at a number of options other than going back to school ... the most attractive being a return to the ski business at Killington.

I say "return" because during my senior year at Middlebury College, I had worked as a bartender at Killington, bringing in much-needed cash (I was a scholarship and ROTC kid). I got to know many of the resort managers, and when, just prior to Christmas 1969, I got my notice to report to Ft. Gordon, Georgia, in late February 1970, it made no sense to start a new semester. So off I went to Killington, looking for a way to bridge the gap to my reporting date.

I distinctly remember sitting at the bar at the Wobbly Barn (one of my college bartending venues and one of the most iconic après-ski joints in America ... to this day) and talking to the owner, Jack Giguere. I was whining a bit about the recent turn of events, having convinced myself that by remaining in graduate school the war would end and I would face only "reserve" duty. Sitting next to us was Foster T. Chandler, Killington's soft-spoken, almost-reclusive VP of marketing. Foster had been listening in and asked me to come see him the next morning. Well, there are some advantages to being an English major. Foster needed someone to help with cranking out resort newsletters, writing SOPs for the growing central-reservations business, and other tasks. Just by being in the right place at the right time, I was hired to assist him over the holidays ... at $25 a day plus free skiing. Such a deal!

Another lucky break occurred when my reporting date was pushed back, first to June, and then eventually to the fall. Foster kept me on through that entire period, and was an incredibly patient tutor. I had zero business experience. Killington was growing by leaps and bounds, and we all seemed to be taking it in "on the fly." On March 17, Saint Patrick's Day, I went into my office to find a note from Foster ("FTC"). That note told me:

- I haven't had a vacation in years.

- I'm gone and will come back, but don't know when.

- Pres (Preston Smith, company president) knows how to reach me.

- You're in charge ... Talk to Pres if you feel you're getting in over your head.

- Good luck.

Wow. I ran into the mailroom and showed the note to Norma Biathrow and Betty Merrill (two longtime marketing staffers). They laughed and said, basically, "Lord help us now." I was 23.

Pres did stop in from time to time, mostly to offer some edits relative to my snow report. But I was left to my own devices to figure things out. Surviving probably equated to success. That experience of working with Foster gave me skills that I never would have developed, a level 101 understanding for the business of skiing, and a deep appreciation of the culture that was or was becoming Killington, which was then ranked in the top five nationally for visitation and at least that high in terms of stature.

I should add that Foster at that time was arguably the most respected and talented marketer in the ski business. I remember his "purple prose" ad, a full-page invitation to join the ranks of skiers (the full text of "A Little Bit of Purple Prose About Learning To Ski" is reprinted in the Appendix). Foster ran the ad in the likes of *Time, Newsweek, Sports Illustrated, The New Yorker, Glamour, Mademoiselle, National Geographic,* and even *Seventeen.* He backed these up with full-page spreads in the major dailies. I was reminiscing with him recently about those days gone by when he said, in his typical fashion, "Well, Christopher, people will buy what you sell them." He knew back then what the company wanted to sell, and put together the plan to do just that. And it worked.

I'll never forget Killington's "Sunday Night Registration," where many in management pitched in to get a thousand new participants registered, outfitted, and oriented for their Monday first-timer experience. By today's standards, the process was clumsy and intimidating. But at the time, Foster and others were applying the rules of process efficiency to a business that had never focused on that sort of discipline. Killington's decades-long leadership in "learn-to-ski" encouraged other resorts to develop similar programs, and helped position skiing as one of the most vibrant participation sports in the country. A sport that, despite periodic doomsayers, enjoys record attendance and appeal to this day.

No question, my experience with Foster helped me with my interview with Pres Smith some two years later. The position was a new one. It certainly sounded attractive, and would buy me some time to figure out "what's next" in my life.

That first day on the job is really where my learning and understanding of the ski business began.

DAY ONE, OCTOBER 20, 1972

The Killington Corporate Offices were located next to the maintenance and snowmaking facilities, at the far end of the Killington Peak parking lot. "Modest" understates how basic the building was: a two-story, cinder-block construction. Some offices had threadbare carpeting, but the more general floor treatments were concrete or painted plywood. I knew what to expect, given my earlier tour of duty with Foster Chandler. Pres invested on the mountain, where the guest would be impacted. Offices were not a priority.

I was shown my new work space between Pres and the VP of finance, Marty Wilson, and then introduced to Les Otten, who was heading out the door to Sunday River, Maine, a small ski area that Killington had just purchased. Otten had participated in Killington's "Management Training Program" the prior year. With that experience, a keen intelligence, and a degree from Ithaca College, he was offered a position at Sunday River as assistant general manager, and became GM some eight months later.

Smith was an intimidating presence. Well over 6 feet, he was almost always the tallest man in the room. Blond-haired and handsome, with a kind of fiery intensity, even when "relaxed" he was something of a slow burn.

We started chatting, and I realized that while he had spoken during my earlier interview about "environmental" issues he needed help with, we really hadn't put much definition to the job I was starting.

I asked if he had a job description. He had his feet up on his desk (not unusual) and gave me his classic, intense stare. Then, "I want you to sit in that chair every day this week, listen to every conversation I have, sit in on every meeting. If I have to leave for other business, you'll come with me. If after this week, you think you need a job description, give it to me Monday."

Then he reached over to his stack of lined, legal writing pads and tossed one at me. He was a fan of No. 2 pencils, and asked if I needed one. I replied "No," said I had a pen. That led to a lengthy dissertation on the advantages of No. 2 pencils versus pens. "You can always change your mind and use the eraser…" My education had begun. So 8 to 5, or longer, each day, I sat and listened. I don't believe I ever got a job description.

One of the things that made the Killington decision an easy one for me was that I didn't have a lodging issue. My friend, Jack Giguere, après-ski impresario, had recently separated from his wife, Phoebe. Jack invited Vinny Donnelly, who was managing Jack's Charity's pub operation, and me to be roommates at his Summit Drive home. Vinny and I took rooms in the basement, but it was quite luxurious, at least compared to any other options. "Bachelors Three," Jack called it. When I got back to the house after that first day at work, Jack asked how it had gone. I gave a brief recap, and Jack noted, "I don't always agree with Pres, but it seems like you just picked a great boss."

Pres Smith absolutely defined the Killington culture in those early years. He had assembled a very talented management team and drove them to innovate in every way. He challenged every existing standard of ski-area operations. Rather than bringing in consultants, he would always opt for in-house development, whether it was land planning, snowmaking, trail design, financial systems, whatever. And he was a master at creating a sense of urgency. Things got done, generally on time and on budget, and always in a unique "Killington way."

In the early '70s, most resorts were still using a European model of instruction, with the venerable "Hans" or "Karl," the stereotypical Austrian or Swiss ski school veterans, barking "follow me and bend zee knees." By contrast, Killington's ski school was a virtual production line, led by Leo Denis, a talented engineer whom Pres recruited from Howe Scale in nearby Rutland. Leo was as competent as he was unassuming, capable of managing complex construction projects in the off-season.

Prior to Leo's appointment as the VP-Skiing, Killington's ski school had been led by Austrian Karl Pfeiffer. Leo became responsible for converting the school to a very American-focused teaching strategy. (One of the early directors he hired was Peter Duke, a member of PSIA's National Demo Team, one of the highest honors an instructor can receive. It was at Killington that Peter met his future wife, Patty. The two of them went on to found Smartwool, the incredibly successful, high-end sports sock and apparel company. They eventually sold their interest and about five years later founded Point6, a next-generation sock company. I met Peter and Patty during their Killington tenure, and we rekindled our old friendship in Steamboat, where they had eventually settled and where Point6 makes its home. Small world.)

Killington was teaching skiing to absolute beginners using graduated-length skis, starting out with 3-footers and moving up to longer skis as competence rose. *SKI* Magazine had introduced the teaching program, called GLM (Graduated Length Method), but Leo Denis, in the "Killington Way," put his own stamp on it.

At Killington, GLM became the "Accelerated Ski Method." And accelerated it was. Taught in five-day midweek and two-day weekend sessions, Leo's team of instructors moved *thousands* through the learning process. Killington was blessed with an ideal teaching slope, isolated from the bustle of the rest of the resort. First-timers would be shuttled to an assembly area below the Killington Base Lodge and work their way down toward the base of Snowshed on a trail reserved for instruction. This might have been one of the original terrain gardens! Key to Killington's strategy was eliminating fear or intimidation, so new skiers learned the very basics before ever riding a lift. In fact, at the bottom of the learning trail there was a practice chairlift to simulate the loading and unloading process. Students then moved on to the Snowshed slope, which had a gentle grade and wide, three-quarters-of-a-mile-long slopes, plus three double chairlifts. Killington had 999 pairs of the short skis, so that determined the maximum number of students. Imagine a thousand new skiers every day (in the five-day midweek and two-day weekend programs), plus another 4,000 on different vacation packages, some with lessons and some lifts only. The average midweek crowd was 7,500, once you added in day-trippers and pass-holders. Weekends would see almost double that number. To my knowledge, no ski area in the country was doing these kinds of numbers in the "learn-to" segment, and few were doing more total visits. As for those new skiers, they were very satisfied with the experience and most joined the ranks of committed skiers. As a special perk, graduates could purchase the skis, boots, and poles for as little as $99 (my recollection) at the end of the week. Many did. In our industry today, it has been estimated that only 15 percent of new skiers actually stay with the sport. If those numbers are to be believed, Killington was indeed ahead of its time as a new-skier factory, given its processes for successful introduction versus the industry average.

While most resorts at the time were heavy users of the National Ski Patrol–trained volunteers, Pres was one of the first to transition to an "all-paid" Patrol. He had a political conservative's understandable paranoia relative to unions, and no doubt anticipated eventual unionizing efforts from patrols and other emergency-service providers. Many of the new "paid" positions transitioned to construction or maintenance positions in the summer. Pres was very focused on maintaining an effective year-round staff. Specialized skills, like lift evacuations, were not left just to patrol. He insisted that all physically capable office staff were trained in evacuation, even nighttime steep-cable evacuation on the gondola. In that way, in the event of an evacuation, personnel not critical to the operation could carry the load, leaving patrol to continue with normal duties at the ski area. He also wanted patrollers to be cross-trained to perform lift relief.

Perhaps nothing expressed the Killington Way more than its snowmaking strategy. Pres believed that Eastern skiers were so passionate and committed that they would ski even short patches of marginal snow if that product managed to extend the season. So Killington would, for decades, be the first to open and last to close in the East. In many years, it was the first to open nationally.

If there was a window of cold weather in early October, the snowguns would be cranked on. As soon as a skiable patch could be laid down, Killington would open. In the 1970s, this entailed skiing about 2,000 linear feet of Upper Cascade, and riding the Killington double chairlift down at the end of the day. It was not unusual for skiers to enjoy a few runs on Columbus Day weekend, while the foliage was still hanging on. Foster Chandler would have his PR machine cranked up and very soon, images of skiing, the first of the year, would flood the media. More often than not, the ski area had to close as warm, New England weather returned. But the message was out there. "We're open." And for the few hundred skiers who traveled to enjoy the early snow, it was a memorable experience.

Snowmaking technology was in its infancy in those days. The Killington system used a combination of permanent electrical compressors, augmented by a fleet of rented, diesel compressors to provide the compressed air needed to mix with water to make snow. The quality of that compressed air was warm and moist, and when it interacted with New England humidity ... well, it wasn't always the finest product. The snow surface was often "bulletproof." When temperatures were very cold, the product could be excellent, but for the most part, it was a hard, unforgiving surface.

I REMEMBER HEADING UP THE MOUNTAIN one late May morning with Leo Denis to see how the snow was holding up. It was classic Vermont mud season, warm and foggy. We walked from the top of the Killington double chair to the Glades area, where the Glades Triple had been providing late-season skiing on one run. There was more mud than snow. So Leo and I headed back to Foster's office with the bad news. Leo was describing the conditions and the reality that it was time to close for the season. Foster looked up from his type-writer and yelled, "Norma (Biathrow), cut the tapes!" (Translation: End the snow report.) He went back to his typewriter without another word to us. As I look back, this was a classic Killington moment. Another long season—more than 200 operating days—was over. Time to move on.

But it was really all that we, as skiers, knew in those days. And unlike the modern ski resort, the grooming equipment available back then didn't allow this "firm" surface to be renovated. We had "powder makers" that were dragged behind snowcats. They created a loose surface about 1-inch thick. Nice for a few runs but then quickly "skied off." The ice layer would remain unless covered with prodigious amounts of natural snow, something that was not a regular occurrence in the East.

My friend Michael Berry, the longtime NSAA president, often says, "If you are nostalgic for the good old days, you were not there." That is so true in terms of the quality of the snow surface and the lift systems as well. Remember the surface lifts (T-Bars and Pomas) or slow, fixed-grip chairlifts of yesteryear versus today's high-speed detachables, some with bubble covers to protect from the cold, and others even featuring heated seats.

THE ORIGINAL CAPITAL that started the Killington train at its founding in 1956 came from Hartford, Connecticut. Joseph D. Sargent, a prominent financial executive with Conning & Co., was a key early investor and became chairman of the board. The company was Sherburne Corporation (named after the town of Sherburne, where Killington was located). Joe and Pres enjoyed a 40-year partnership, with Joe providing strategic financial leadership throughout that time. A Yale graduate with a degree in economics, he was the ultimate metrics guy, designing all of Killington's financial reporting systems. At the time, most ski resorts were led by former ski racers, 10th Mountain Division veterans, or just passionate enthusiasts for the sport. Joe Sargent was an anomaly.

Few operated with the kind of financial tools and discipline that Joe Sargent established for Killington. As an example of his passion for detail, Joe created a chart of accounts that provided separate codes not just for each lift, but for key components of the lift. At one point, I remember him arguing that we should track expenses by lift tower (sheave replacements, etc.). While some of this was over the top, it created a company-wide attention to detail that set the organization up for year after year of profitable operations. These were actual after-tax profits, not just positive EBITDA (Earnings Before Interest, Taxes, Depreciation, and Amortization, it provides a baseline for a company's operating profitability). There wasn't much need to worry about interest costs: there were virtually none. The company sold subordinated debentures most years with an interest rate below market because they included skiing privileges. The only other debt in place was a line of credit with Bank of Boston . . . and this was almost always paid off by midwinter. Not exactly a leveraged company.

The weekly management meeting was held at 7:30 every Thursday morning in the basement of the Killington Base Lodge, in a bar called the Cellar Door Lounge. Bar tables were pulled together for a pseudo roundtable and then, for the next hour or two, imbued with the strong odor of stale beer, the team would review the prior week's financials. Computer spreadsheets covered the table and detailed the performance of all revenue centers and all operating departments by manager, so it was clear where accountability lay. These reports provided more accurate information on a weekly basis than I enjoyed some 40 years later (when the focus had shifted to monthly reporting). Constant attention to the basic metrics of the business made everyone a better manager. Toward the end of the meeting, Foster provided his forecast for levels of business for the next 10 days. Any special events or weather issues were covered. And then the meeting was over. While Joe Sargent never attended these sessions, he was certainly present in spirit. We'd leave and the bar would open for the day.

Joe left Hartford every Friday night for the three-plus-hour drive during the winter season. He didn't have his own office or administrative assistant at Killington. He'd park himself in Pres' office every weekend and winter holiday period, working on budgets, system designs, capital planning, etc. In the 1970s, the only time I ever saw Joe take a vacation was in the spring when he and his wife, Mary, headed to St. John. I don't think I've ever known an executive with a comparable work ethic.

Overseeing the day-to-day financial activities, and subject to frequent visits and coaching from Joe, was Martel D. Wilson Jr., aka Marty Wilson, or MDW. Marty was of the generation that still dealt with the awful reality of polio and, as a result, had one leg shorter than the other and an ankle that was fairly frozen. He walked with an obvious limp, but never let that modify his lifestyle. A talented water-skier, he often used a mono ski on the slopes. Marty also shared Pres' passion for creative, independent thinking and for challenging the status quo. He was also a notorious penny-pincher. At a time when small, electronic calculators were becoming available, Marty still had a slide ruler on his desk, next to a mechanical punch calculator. Younger readers will probably need to Google these financial instruments.

One of my unrealized passions at the time was to learn how to sail. I never had that opportunity growing up, but something about blue water and white sails was immensely appealing to me. Marty, along with his partner and Killington's assistant controller, Bob Fenner, had a boat that he kept with a charter company in the Virgin Islands. He had also raced sailboats growing up. So one day over lunch, I asked Marty how I would go about learning to sail. His response: "Read a book."

When I arrived at work the next morning, there was a stack of books on sailing in a neat, high pile on my desk. About midmorning, he dropped by to tell me there were more I should read when I finished the current pile. That day was the beginning for me of a lifetime of sailboat racing, and the experiences and friendship that evolved from racing have added incredible richness to my life. Marty Wilson taught me many things, but most importantly, "You can do anything you want, if you just put your mind to it . . . and read a book."

The Killington senior management team was quite the collection of type A personalities. Slow decision-making was never an issue. If anything, we probably charged into the battle a little too quickly from time to time, particularly on the political or environmental front. Pres was a very conservative Republican and resented any outside interference in the business of Killington. This made for spectacular fireworks as Vermont began shifting toward a more progressive-leaning political environment.

WITH THE FORCE OF THOSE PERSONALITIES and the conservative tendencies of the entire team, it always amazed me how fundamentally inclusive the culture was in those days. When Killington met its financial goals for the fiscal year, a bonus would be distributed based on that success. In many years, that was as much as six-weeks' pay for all full-time, year-round employees. Lift mechanic or company president, the formula was the same.

Pres' visibility in the organization and his willingness to take on any task or role created a culture where everyone was expected to pitch in wherever needed. In those days, parking and traffic were quite the issue. Killington experienced such volume on weekends and holidays that the 5-mile-long Killington Road became a virtual parking lot at the end of the day. Many of us assisted in making the best out of the situation by directing traffic. At the end of a very long day, it wasn't unusual to find a group of mangers and mechanics sitting on the floor in Lift Maintenance Supervisor Wayne Smith's office, where a few beers and a bottle of Jack Daniel's were usually available (verboten in the modern world). While everyone was probably anxious to get home, there was no griping, just time spent sharing stories and, generally, feeling good about work and life.

Wayne worked for Dave Wilcox, the VP of maintenance and one of the most approachable executives I'd ever met. He was another Howe Scale engineer, as I recollect, now starting a career in the ski business. Wilcox was a hockey fan. I can't remember if it was originally his idea, but out of those evenings in Wayne's office came the idea that we should have the hockey-game-to-end-all-hockey-games. On Snowshed Pond at the base of the ski area, we would create a hockey rink and play a game under the lights: management on one team; non-management on the other.

Snowshed Pond turned out to be a less than great idea. It served as the main snowmaking storage pond, and as a result, the actual water level could be well below the ice surface, depending on the time of year.

The morning after the scheduled evening "clearing" project on the pond, I drove in to work, and there was the Michigan Loader (aka "The Goose") almost completely submerged.

Wilcox, who I think was driving The Goose that night, presented Pres with the bad news. The Goose was out of service for a while. To his credit, Pres didn't lecture or, worse, cancel the hockey game. But all agreed we had to find another location. As I remember, and probably important for context, this was a challenging time in terms of the business and company morale: the Arab oil embargo meant many guests couldn't get the fuel to make the trip to Vermont. Or it was such a hassle that some just decided to forgo skiing.

The only place we could find that was somewhat flat and with water and power available was next to the sewage treatment plant. Using treated, reclaimed water, we spent several nights making the ice, building nets, and generally "cobbling" together rink boards that would (barely) keep the puck on the ice and define the playing area. Company electricians rigged the temporary lighting. Somehow, spectator stands appeared . . . borrowed from somewhere. Ed McDonald, a longtime maintenance employee and town selectman, played goalie for his team. He didn't have any goalie pads, so he made his own out of plywood, pipe insulation, and duct tape. He was a vision. In deference to his equipment, or lack thereof, we agreed to no slap shots.

The night of the game was warm and foggy. The ice surface, which I would describe as "poor to fair" to start the game, deteriorated quickly. No matter. I have no idea who won. It was hilarious and a good time was had by all, notwithstanding a few injuries and too much beer consumed after the game. Eddie Danks, the manager of Snowshed Lodge and a former Cornell hockey star, blew out his knee. This was the first, and last, employee hockey game at the sewage treatment plant. That said, as a result of "the game," we did form our own Killington team and join the Rutland Amateur Hockey Association's adult league. We had great fun for many years.

I'VE BEEN FORTUNATE to work with some great teams over the past 40-plus years, but in terms of inclusiveness and camaraderie, I can't say that I ever experienced anything that matched Killington in the 1970s.

Not that there weren't issues, especially in terms of guest service. Pres and his talented lift manager, Hank Lunde (later president of Killington and Stowe), were fanatical about lift efficiency. "Load every chair to capacity, and try to never stop or slow the lift" was their mantra. Monitoring equipment was in place so Hank could track every stop and slow by lift. He even had the company dispatcher, the aforementioned Ed McDonald, monitor conversations of lift operators to ensure attentiveness. It would drive Hank nuts that as soon as he loaded a chairlift, the bottom operator would call the top to advise that "the boss" was on his way up. So Ed was supposed to make sure that didn't happen. As a company, we hadn't learned that it's best to catch someone doing the right thing and celebrate that.

For the many New Yorkers in the lift lines, the push for efficiency was just an extension of their world, and probably appreciated. For everyone else, it felt as though they were being herded up the hill. We would hear occasional "mooing" from those in the lift maze. The company culture defined service in terms of how quickly skiers got up the hill, not how they "felt" about that experience.

Customer feedback came via "complaint forms" available at the base-lodge information desks. Used or unused lift tickets were invariably stapled to the forms. It would not be unusual to have hundreds of these collected on busy days, especially if the weather turned bad. While they were all answered, most were done so by form letter. It just wasn't part of the culture to dig deeper on guest relations.

Pres was one of the few guys who could manage the malfunction junction that was the intersection of the Killington Road and the RamsHead and Snowshed parking lots. Heavy traffic streaming down from the Upper Killington parking lot would have to slow as numerous turning movements occurred at that spot. Pres would stand in the middle of the road, no uniform or fluorescent vest (probably hadn't been invented yet!), and try to keep some order to the chaos. I remember helping out one day when a driver heading down the hill ignored Pres and his instructions to stop. Pres chased the fellow down the road, somehow got a hold of the steering wheel, and next thing I knew, the offending car and Pres were in the ditch together and Pres was dragging the driver out the door. Our grooming supervisor, Royal Biathrow, was town constable in those days, so I don't recall any consequences.

IN A BRIEF SEGUE TO MY PERSONAL LIFE during those early years: I had moved in with Jack Giguere and Vinny Donnelly. Jack had said, "Bachelors Three." Well, I think that had lasted about three days when Sally West, Vinny's girlfriend, arrived with her luggage. Jack was a notorious romancer, but quickly found his match in a young Terry Jones. She didn't move in right away, but the handwriting was on the wall. It was getting crowded, not to mention that the band from the night before at the Wobbly Barn would often be sleeping on the living room floor. There was never a dull moment. It was like being back in my college fraternity, but I was the only guy who had to get up each morning.

So I rented the downstairs apartment in Bob Perry's house. Bob was a talented senior film and media guy with Western Electric in New York. He made the weekend trip from Manhattan every week of the year and was Killington's still- and motion-picture talent. His posters from that era are still collector's items among the winter-sports crowd. Bob was also well-connected with AP and UPI executives and had a talent for getting his black-and-white photos into mainstream media. To my knowledge, no other resort in New England had a resource like Bob Perry on its marketing team.

When I had worked for Foster Chandler before entering the service, I had the pleasure of working with Bob. As an example of the kind of guy he was, I'll share this story. It was late October 1970, and my plan before arriving in

Ft. Gordon, Georgia, was to drive to Florida for a week's vacation. Bob knew the dates and said that he was going to be in Atlanta the night before my reporting date. He asked if I'd like to join him for dinner. I had always wanted to visit Atlanta, and it was barely out of the way, so I said, "great."

He told me we would have to eat early, as he had business that night, so I said fine. We enjoyed a lovely diner at a French restaurant downtown. As we finished dinner, he said, "Well, you have to go now." I probably looked bewildered as he handed me a ticket to the Muhammad Ali/Jerry Quarry fight about to start across the street at the Atlanta Municipal Auditorium. Row 3, ringside. Bob knew that I was a crazed Ali fan and had put this all together as a surprise. It was a spectacle unlike anything I had ever experienced, as Ali pummeled Quarry for three rounds. That's how long the fight lasted. I'll never forget that night, and Bob Perry's thoughtfulness.

DESPITE SOME HICCUPS (energy crisis, double-digit interest rates), this was a time of amazing growth for skiing and the Killington organization. The company's balance sheet was growing steadily, and it was time to think beyond Killington and the relatively small Maine adventure. Mount Snow, southern Vermont's largest ski area, was in bankruptcy in 1977. It seemed like a logical acquisition target for the Sherburne Corporation.

CHAPTER 2

Mount Snow Acquisition:

A Chance to Lead

M ount Snow, located in southern Vermont between Bennington and Brattleboro, and Stowe, to the far north, were the early beneficiaries of the rapid growth of New England skiing. Walter Schoenknecht, the visionary force behind Mount Snow, opened the ski area in 1954. Just about everything he did was contrary to prevailing views on how a resort should be developed. Like Pres Smith, he disdained professional consultants, especially architects, preferring to sketch his vision in the parking lot gravel and then just let the work begin.

The construction techniques used to build the four-story central core of his main base lodge resulted in a structure so unstable that vertical, steel supports had to be added on the north and south walls to keep the building from falling over. Walt was so intent on preserving the sense of open space in his Sundance Lodge (a half-mile south of the main base area) that he eliminated appropriate interior, vertical supports for the roof, which, of course, proceeded to begin slowly settling under the snowload. He jury-rigged a complex cabling system to stabilize the roof, but this too proved inadequate and, eventually, had to be replaced with internal support columns. Obviously, this occurred at a time when there were virtually no building codes in Vermont at the state or local level.

Walter's view of Eastern skiing was that it could not compete with warm-weather beach resorts unless the ski area's environment was designed to remind guests of a warmer clime, while diminishing the reality of cold weather. Given New England's often-below-zero weather, this was a challenge. The design philosophy led to a contradictory, often fun, and sometimes frustrating ski experience. Where Pres Smith epitomized design and organizational discipline, Walter went about developing Mount Snow with an almost irrational, artistic flair.

So this was Mount Snow in the late '60s:

Just outside the main base lodge was a heated pool. Stairs took guests up to the roof of the northern section of the lodge, where there were lounge chairs overlooking the pool with a wall of mirrors behind … all facing south. On any nice day, the pool and sunning areas would be packed. Between the pool and the ski slopes was a glass wall to keep the Vermont wind from interfering with the experience. When the weather was perfect, so was the experience. Unfortunately, the weather was seldom perfect and inside the base lodge, where Walter had used single-pane glass to save money during construction, it was often freezing cold.

There was an ice rink, but it was inside the base lodge—along with various tropical plants. The sit-down restaurant on the fourth floor, Reuben Snow's Tavern, had an area of flowers and plantings and a small pool where frogs would leap around, adding a little excitement to the dining experience. It was just a fun, crazy place.

Walter developed his early lift systems using conveyor technology from the mining industry. The early chairlifts were called "clickety clacks:" they were attached to a conveyor chain that pulled the individual chairs along a steel I beam. This required that lift towers be constructed about every 30 feet. The design kept chairs very close to the ground (to keep steel supports short) and it suffered immense friction loss.

I remember skiing Mount Snow as a 16-year-old and catching a tip in the snow shortly after loading. I was pulled from the chair, but since it was only 5 or 6 feet off the ground, I hung on and made it almost to the top, no worse for the wear. As I later learned, this was not an unusual event.

To deal with the friction loss inherent in a system like this, and to keep everything moving, the I beam required an enormous amount of grease. Walter and his mechanics quickly learned that something had to be done to eliminate the black ooze that would show up on guests' parkas, especially on warm days. So each chair was given a metal cover to keep grease off the skiers.

Walter's tropical winter vision was repeated in one of Vermont's first ski hotels, the Snow Lake Lodge, located across from the snowmaking pond. Snow Lake was notorious for its indoor palm trees, Japanese hot and cold pools, and another crazy lift that took guests from the hotel lobby area to the ski area base. It was called the "Air Car," and looked like something the Jetsons might have flown around in.

At the north end of the lake was a fountain that propelled water up hundreds of feet in the air. This was basically a huge icemaker, and by winter's end, Walt's geyser had frozen into a ski hill with a 350-foot vertical drop. Add a rope tow and a slalom course, and summer race camps prospered into late May.

EVERYTHING ABOUT MOUNT SNOW was contradictory ... but fun. By the time the 1970s arrived, Mount Snow had two gondolas. These were really detachable double chairs with an enclosure. Very comfortable on cold days and faster than fixed-grip lifts, but low capacity and very unreliable during frequent wind events. The longer double chairlifts were called "bubble" chairlifts because they had a plastic shield attached to the restraining bar, effectively protecting skiers from outside snow or cold. Unfortunately, this comfort enhancement came at a cost of reliability and effective capacity due to the added weight.

By 1977, the lack of focus and investment in the basics, especially snowmaking, had put Mount Snow in a precarious position. For the 1970–71 ski season, Mount Snow generated 322,000 skier visits. By 1976–77, that number was 209,000, a dramatic 35 percent decline. New England skiing had been hard hit with the double whammy of several poor snow years and the energy crisis of 1973–74. Skiers, being a hardy lot, did not abandon their sport, but the difficulty in dealing with fuel shortages (remember odd- or even-day fill-ups?) caused pretty much across-the-board declines in visitation. With its huge snowmaking plant, Killington made the best out of these challenging years. When word came that Mount Snow was available, it was time for some serious due diligence.

The debtor in possession of the resort was a REIT, the North American Mortgage Investors (NAMI), along with First Wisconsin Mortgage Trust in second position. Walter Schoenknecht and his investors had been through foreclosure and lost everything. By 1977, the Mount Snow management team was reporting directly to a representative for NAMI, and he was looking for buyers. Walt had always kept an apartment in Snow Lake, but one day during that summer he arrived to find his personal effects unceremoniously emptied from his rooms and, literally, dumped on the curb.

When Walt heard of our potential interest, he supported the Killington efforts, even though he and Pres Smith were on different planets. Pres knew that there wouldn't be a role for Walt as he was, clearly, the main contributing agent to the company's troubles. The ski world had changed since Walt's early successes. Financial discipline, so central to Pres' nature, was simply absent in Walt's. They would never be able to work together.

At the time, there were few companies trying to acquire ski resorts. Mount Snow's neighbor to the north, Stratton, had no ambitions beyond providing a great product for its Connecticut gold coast customers. Okemo was a minor player (the Muellers hadn't yet affected their transformation). Stowe remained comfortably positioned somewhere on the large balance sheet of AIG. Ski areas in New York were largely owned by the state. Resorts in New Hampshire and Maine were struggling with the same weather and business problems that had plagued Mount Snow. Likewise, no Western resort that I'm familiar with was looking to acquire Mount Snow or any Eastern resort. There weren't a lot of buyers.

Despite some poor snow years and the energy crisis, the late 1970s and early '80s were actually the "golden years" of Eastern skiing. The sport was growing in popularity. The East was a huge market. And frankly, most of our guests simply hadn't discovered the West. When that began to happen, the ski world changed . . . but that's a later story.

I WAS GIVEN THE JOB of leading the on-the-ground due diligence effort. As noted earlier, Pres Smith had a very conservative business philosophy matched by an equally conservative political worldview. He was very concerned that our efforts to acquire the property would be affected if word somehow leaked out. So we were almost paranoid about secrecy. In retrospect, we were terribly unsophisticated, but we figured out how to quantify most of the issues.

The biggest one was relative to water supply, as employees and Mount Snow business folks relayed that snowmaking was often halted due to lack of water. Pres was concerned enough that we did several cross sections of Snow

Lake to chart its depths and calculate the actual storage capacity. Leo Denis was "lead paddler" in the effort. Of course, this had to occur at night.

The evening in question happened to be the annual gathering of the "Dover Dunkers," a collection of local canoeing and kayaking characters. They had a band set up in the SnowBarn parking lot, adjacent to Snow Lake. We were just within earshot and heard emcee Tiger Miller, the golf course super-intendent and lift manager, announce the coronation of this year's Miss Low Tide! The belle of the ball was Louise McDevitt, girlfriend of Scott Pierpont, a young Mount Snow ski patroller and now well-known industry executive (former president of Mount Snow and The Canyons). Mount Snow was going to be a memorable adventure, indeed.

It turned out that Snow Lake was probably large enough for current needs. Leo's analysis revealed that sediment had settled in the area around the intake pumps, effectively creating a pond within the pond. To fix this would simply require dredging.

THE ON-SITE DILIGENCE WENT QUITE WELL, helped by input from Mount Snow's senior sales manager, John Clifford. John provided introductions to key local business folks and helped lay the groundwork for a smooth transition once the sale was finalized. In terms of an acquisition candidate, Mount Snow was virtually ideal for Killington. Its weaknesses (snowmaking, lift systems and marketing) were Killington's sweet spot. It was a great mountain, and despite some building and structural issues, the resort and surrounding community were capable of significant growth once the weaknesses were addressed.

Negotiations with NAMI took place in the law offices of Ryan, Smith and Carbine in Rutland. John Carbine was a director of the company, and his firm performed general counsel work. The deal was fairly straightforward in that it would be a transfer of assets into a new company (Dover Corporation) that would be a wholly owned subsidiary of Sherburne Corporation (Killington). I was there as keeper of the due diligence material, and witnessed some tense sessions. I vividly remember Pres breaking his No. 2 pencil several times and coming right to the edge of cancelling the deal. John Carbine managed these moments artfully, allowing tempers to calm down and, eventually, bringing the discussions back on track.

On August 8, 1977, the deal closed, and I was offered the opportunity to move to Mount Snow as general manager. This was a wonderful opportunity on several levels. I knew that Pres would allow a reasonable amount of independence in how the resort would be managed and developed. I would also have access to resources at Killington to ensure success. Managing those Killington relationships would prove as important as developing the local management team.

The decision to move wasn't without challenges. My girlfriend and later wife, Eileen, had moved to Killington from Nyack, New York, that summer, and accepted a teaching job in nearby Bridgewater. She agreed to make the move to Mount Snow and was, fortunately, able to get a teaching job in Dover. At one point that summer, waiting to learn whether I was headed to Mount Snow, she had three teaching jobs lined up.

One of the first challenges was where to live. Working with a local realtor, I found a chalet on the Dover Hill Road. It was a typical ski house, with lots of beds and bedrooms on the first floor, a large kitchen/dining area upstairs, and a master bedroom. It was to function as our residence, but also as something of a clubhouse for visiting Killington staff. Pres said, "I'll get the rent if you get the utilities." It was electric heat. Let's just say that he cut a good deal. I paid more for the utilities than the company did for rent. Not the first or last time I found myself at the short end in negotiating with Mr. Smith.

In the early going, it took a huge, collaborative effort. Basically, the entire Killington management team had some role in the construction or operation in those early years. Hank Lunde, Killington's vice president, provided leadership in navigating Vermont's new and complex permitting structure, Act 250. Dave Wilcox helped with snowmaking, lift, and maintenance projects, and Leo Denis with learn-to-ski programs. Foster Chandler basically assumed the role of marketing director, alongside his Killington duties.

PRES WAS VERY CLEAR about what needed to be accomplished before winter set in. Philosophically, the resort needed to be transformed into an efficient, skier-focused facility, and then investments would follow in future years to make the resort a competitive destination for skiers. That would be the marketing message.

In terms of priority projects, lift reliability and capacity needed improvement. That meant the "bubbles" on the major double chairs had to be removed. The Jetson's Air Car from Snow Lake Lodge was to be removed as well. The snowmaking system was woefully inadequate, but given the amount of time until winter, we were handicapped. That said, snowmaking pipelines were extended along the Upper Canyon Trail, providing access to the summit for the first time. Pumps and compressors were updated, and a dragline arrived to start the dredging work on Snow Lake. This project proved challenging, as Vermont had new rules regarding such work, and we had begun without appropriate permits. It was stop and go, but the work got done, thanks to Dave Wilcox's effective negotiating with the State of Vermont.

I mentioned earlier how crazily some of the buildings had been constructed. Well, they also were painted (orange, blue, and white) in a manner that enhanced the craziness. This drove Pres nuts. He had a very strong aesthetic relative to blending the built environment into the surrounding landscape. In other words, we had to repaint virtually every structure as quickly as possible using more subtle, natural colors. Inside Snow Lake Lodge, the natural wood in the lobby area had been painted over. So a local painting contractor from Newfane was hired to strip and restain the interior surfaces. That contractor was a young Stephan Morse, later Speaker of the Vermont House of Representatives. Another team was put to work on deferred maintenance, particularly in the various base lodges. The ice rink went away to create a needed seating area in the main base lodge. And outside, the heated pool rode into the history books. Ditto for the mirror wall, which was failing structurally, along with the stairs that took skiers to that former "sunning" area. Pres didn't want anyone confused about the fact that skiing was now the priority.

Joining me from Killington was Bruce McCloy. Bruce had held a number of roles, most recently that of ski vacation coordinator. He had started in Ski School, and was the logical choice to get the resort's destination vacation business back on track. Eventually, Bruce took over the resort's marketing functions. Foster Chandler had taken the very successful "Accelerated" ski teaching model and created the Killington School for Tennis. Bruce had been involved with constructing the tennis facilities and getting the program rolling.

Which brings me to golf. Golf?

The Mount Snow purchase included an 18-hole, Geoffrey Cornish-designed golf course and an airport adjacent to the course. Both were relative afterthoughts in the acquisition, in the sense that very little value was ascribed to them. I do remember looking at the course during due diligence (it had the usual Vermont issues of too much bedrock and poor drainage). I learned that it was a typical golf operation where the pro shop was managed by the resident pro, Jay Morelli. The pro operated the shop and took revenue from teaching, but the resort kept the greens fees.

When the closing day finally arrived and I settled into Mount Snow, I went looking for Jay. He was in Pebble Beach, having secured a spot in the U.S. Open. Pretty impressive. He finally returned a week or so later, and we met. The golf operation was modest. It was open to the public, and without a large population base (year-round residents in the Dover/Wilmington area probably totaled 3,000), it had to rely on destination golfers. Given the lack of summer marketing by Mount Snow in the preceding years, the golf operation was struggling.

Sometime that fall, Jay, Bruce, and I were talking about how to grow the business. Bruce, given his tennis experience, popped the idea: "Why not do a golf school?" And so was born the Mount Snow Golf School, which opened the following summer. Golf was becoming a hot sport, and our product (five-day midweek and two-day weekend packages) was priced to meet the middle market. Within a few years, we were actually generating more revenue from golf lessons than ski lessons.

Jay Morelli now owns the school, having acquired it from Mount Snow, including a satellite winter operation in Crystal River, Florida. He has successfully ridden the ups and downs of golf's appeal (not to mention ownership changes at Mount Snow) through the years.

His impact during the early years of Killington's ownership went beyond golf. For a while, he worked winter seasons in various non-golf capacities. His passion being golf, he was a duck out of water ... and not truly happy until we opened the winter school in Florida. But he was a master at customer service and led our organization by example. His success came from a natural warmth, immediate likeability, and a strong desire to avoid conflict. Problems were resolved on the spot when Jay was involved. Those of us from the Killington organization were trained as production engineers. In many cases, we lacked the softer skills the service business was beginning to expect. I think Jay Morelli set Mount Snow up for long-term success by setting the example for its service culture. He does it to this day.

WHICH BRINGS ME TO A BRUCE MCCLOY SEGUE. A few years into new ownership, we had constructed a 7,200-foot, fixed-grip triple chair to replace the old Lift 7. This was another bad idea in terms of it being just too long for a fixed-grip lift (a 15-minute ride time, not counting stops or slows) and again it was the wrong manufacturer: Yan. Just a few days after opening the new lift, the gearbox seized up, and we were forced to evacuate. Fortunately, we were well-trained and had a large number of staff members immediately deployed, with the result that all were safely off the lift in little more than an hour.

Bruce, by this time, was overseeing marketing and customer relations. He was incredibly patient, even with some "regulars" who took advantage of his accessibility. One of those was a Mrs. Berger. She was notorious for barging into the third-floor office area and just yelling for Bruce. This was a regular event, as she had multitudinous complaints that Bruce patiently listened to. I could often hear her calling for Bruce, even though my office was at the other end of the hall.

The day after the evacuation, Mrs. Berger presented herself at the front desk. Bruce met with her and heard the following: "You should be ashamed of yourselves with what happened yesterday. It was truly an awful experience for all of us involved. And to make matters worse, I was in the same chair with my friend Gloria, and when we got to the ground, your people gave her a free pass, but ignored me."

Bruce simply smiled and said, "Mrs. Berger, you just made my day. I personally evacuated Gloria yesterday, and you were not with her." At that, she spun on her heels and left the office. Bruce probably used that story as a reminder that, while we always assume the guest is right, that isn't always the case.

GIVEN THE CHALLENGES Mount Snow had faced in the previous seven years, it was not a surprise to confirm that the management team had little depth. Shortly after the closing, the president, Phil Saluter, departed along with several marketing staffers who had worked with him when he had held the title of marketing director. The mountain manager was on vacation when we closed and, as I recollect, headed to a new job in Canada, perhaps recognizing that he would not be a good fit with the new company. This left a significant void in the organization, given the sheer volume of work that had to occur in preparation for the ski season. To make sure the construction projects were completed on time and on budget, we needed to add staff quickly. Fortunately, several key maintenance/snowmaking supervisors from Killington took on the challenge, and many remained. I think of Jim Fifield in lift maintenance and Fred Baker for snowmaking.

Most of the bases were covered as we headed into fall. Tiger Miller, who doubled as lift manager and golf course maintenance supervisor, stayed on. The weak link was leadership in other mountain operations areas. We were also relying on Killington staff for construction supervision and sorely needed local talent in that area.

We did learn that one area of strength was ski patrol, which had a veteran paid and volunteer staff. Additionally, its Base First Aid facility provided a physician on premises throughout the winter season. Dr. Mickey Wolf, who operated the clinic, was one of the most respected ski trauma doctors in Vermont. The ability to treat injured skiers on-site was critical, given the almost hour-long ride to the closest regional hospitals (Brattleboro and Bennington).

The patrol was led by David Buckley, who had worked seasonally in that role for several years. We were all impressed with Buckley's knowledge of the mountain, lack of ego, and heavy construction experience. He had operated his own, successful excavation company during the off-season, but agreed to come to work for us full-time and oversee the mountain operations (except lifts). Eventually, he would become the VP of mountain operations.

Never happier than when he was operating or directing large excavation equipment, Buckley thrived on the fast-paced construction activity that was occurring that fall and early winter. His knowledge of snowmaking was limited, but he quickly grasped the operation and made immediate improvements. I don't think anyone was more critical to our early successes than Buckley. He was a natural management talent and a great bridge among all the new Killington people, myself included, and the longtime Mount Snow staff who remained. He was also able to establish a great working relationship with Dave Wilcox at Killington. When, many years later, Sherburne Corporation (now S-K-I Ltd.) bought Goldmine ski area in Southern California (renamed Bear Mountain) and began a massive reconstruction of that facility, it was Buckley and many of his Mount Snow team members who relocated short-term to provide expertise and management oversight.

(Buckley eventually left his positon at Mount Snow. In early December 1996, shortly after opening for the season, we were visited by Les Otten, the new owner. He brought along his right-hand mountain operations man, Burt Mills. Both Buckley and I were proud of how much terrain we had been able to open given the time of year. Les wanted to make a point about the quality of snow he expected. As we got off the old Bear Trap lift, he made it clear that we had no business being satisfied with the product. He was unhappy with the snow quality and proceeded to berate the two of us. It couldn't have been a more awkward moment. I could tell by the look in Buckley's eye that he was checking out. He'd seen enough of Les Otten. David got us through that first year with Les and then moved on. While he has had a number of successful business ventures, he never got back to working full-time in the ski business. What a loss.)

That first season at Mount Snow turned out to be an excellent snow year for the East. From a service perspective, our guests could clearly note the new emphasis on the ski experience. We made some horrific, bulletproof snow on Upper Canyon (the new snowmaking line). But we opened as early as possible and extended the season later than in prior years. Surprisingly, there was little pushback regarding the takeaways (bubble chairs, Air Car, etc.), even from tenured locals. I think they were just relieved to have some financial stability and cut us some slack.

From a financial perspective, it was a home run for Sherburne Corporation. The company reported that consolidated skier visits from its three ski areas exceeded 1 million, with two-thirds of the increase due to the acquisition of Mount Snow (Sunday River was still in the fold). At Mount Snow: "Gross income was up more than 40 percent and ahead of our $4 million expectation, which we mentioned in our last Annual Report." On a consolidated basis, gross income increased 72 percent. These were big numbers for that era and led to continued, significant capital investments at Mount Snow. For the summer of 1978, a new top-to-bottom triple chair was constructed, a learn-to-ski center was established in the Sundance Base Lodge, and the snowmaking system was significantly expanded.

And mistakes were made . . . Snow Lake Lodge guests were not happy with the removal of the Air Car. That decision was certainly related to Pres' insistence on eliminating Walter's "excesses." There were design issues and also capacity issues. We had heard talk of long waits to get to the mountain via the Air Car, aggravating the general issue of lack of capacity with the mountain's ski lifts. Anything that would reduce wait time seemed to be a good idea. That was a mistake. The funky lift was key to the lodging experience at Snow Lake and its clear point of differentiation. Any property could operate a shuttle. Only one lodge had a ski lift in its lobby.

In retrospect, I think we should have tried to keep the outdoor pool. Eventually, space considerations dictated that the lodge be expanded over the pool/patio area, but in the late 1970s, keeping the pool and upgrading that area would have provided some real energy in the base area. Like the Air Car, it was unique for a Vermont ski area and the source of great PR.

Relocating the ski school lift to Sundance and establishing a learn-to-ski center was, in hindsight, not a great move. It was predicated on building the midweek ski vacation business, and that market, for the East, was not growing. Killington was the dominant player and had the most competitive facilities and skiing product. We just couldn't compete to grow the market. Eventually, the learn-to-ski center was returned to its initial location, just north of the main base lodge.

Lack of uphill capacity was the biggest business and service issue. On peak days, guests simply couldn't get in enough runs for a satisfying ski experience. The plan to improve uphill capacity included a 7,300-foot, fixed-grip triple chairlift that would be constructed parallel to the existing G-1 gondola. Our Killington production mentality said, "Why not just run a longer lift and try to make it go as fast as possible."

Two problems: loading efficiency and travel time. Even with extra operators at the bottom, given the range of ability levels trying to use the lift, it stopped frequently for misloads or unloads. Even at peak speed and with no stops or slows, it was a 15-minute ride. Add in a few extra minutes for the stops on a cold, windy day, and that was not a great experience.

In our defense, this was at a time when detachable technology simply wasn't available as a cost-effective solution. That said, using two shorter lifts in tandem to access the summit would have been a better solution. (Mount Snow has since replaced it with the Bluebird Express, a covered, six-seat detachable.) Several years later, we repeated this mistake when replacing the Sundance double with a triple. That lift has since been split into two lifts.

Our second season brought more challenges, as the weather was generally uncooperative. That said, Mount Snow managed to increase skier visits and profitability, and Sherburne Corporation continued to grow at double digits. The company had successfully absorbed Mount Snow and would be on the lookout for other acquisition opportunities.

In October 1980, the company sold its Sunday River Ski Area to its general manager and former Killington Management Trainee, Leslie B. Otten. Otten would begin a dramatic, 15-year expansion of the resort, bringing Sunday River to the forefront of New England skiing. Sherburne Corporation (now a public company, S-K-I Ltd.) would not acquire another resort until January 1988, when it purchased the Goldmine ski area in Southern California.

LOOKING BACK AT THESE EARLY EXPERIENCES at Killington and Mount Snow, there is one clear regret I have relative to their status today as regional resorts versus "what might have been." While the outside perception of the ski business insists that the core financial driver is real estate, nothing could be farther from the truth. Well-run resorts make money on operations. That said, real estate is very important for destination ski resorts in that it can support or enable the strategic vision. I doubt that Vail Resorts generated much net income from its Arrabelle project. Yet that hotel and its amenities were central to Vail's strategy for reenergizing its LionsHead base village. A strategic investment if there ever was one.

Pres Smith and the S-K-I Ltd. board were highly skeptical of real estate, given the higher level of risk and unpredictability. So both Killington and Mount Snow never developed competitive base villages to round out the resort experience. Foster Chandler notes that Killington in the 1970s had 18,000 beds. "Try to find those now," he says. Many were ski dorms or lodges, since torn down or no longer operating. It is beyond the scope of this book, but it would be interesting to track skier days against the "functioning" bed base at Killington and Mount Snow. If anything, it would emphasize how important a modern bed base is to a given resort's success.

In terms of developing new beds, there were regulatory hurdles. We're talking about the State of Vermont. Nonetheless, there were windows of opportunity to reset the base areas at those two resorts, but these were not acted upon. The bottom line: Both now lack the modern beds and amenities desired by current guests. Okemo, Stowe, Stratton, and even Sugarbush have been able to add new beds and improve their competitive position in Vermont. In New Hampshire, Loon's recent success can probably be attributed to bed base growth as much as to the addition of South Mountain.

CHAPTER 3

Then Along Came Les:

The Buying Binge

S-K-I Ltd. had continued its mostly successful string of 34 consecutive profitable years, a track record that today's resort operators might benefit from studying. By 1995, the company had expanded its holdings to include Sugarloaf, Maine (51 percent); Waterville Valley, New Hampshire; and Haystack, Vermont; and sold its erratically performing and cash-consuming Bear Mountain to Fibreboard (owner of Northstar in California).

Even after disposing of Bear, S-K-I Ltd. was one of the largest ski-resort holding companies in the nation. Its NASDAQ-listed stock had been thinly traded in a narrow range for several years when, in the spring of 1996, Les Otten presented the board of directors with an offer to purchase all outstanding stock for $104.6 million, a significant premium to the then-market value of the shares. He wanted a prompt closing with virtually no due diligence. Cash for the purchase would come from his LBO Holdings and the Bank of Boston. The S-K-I board and senior officers controlled about 30 percent of the stock and had been looking for opportunities to exit the business. Pres Smith and Joe Sargent were in their mid-to-late 60s and were ready to move on. The offer was accepted and the deal closed on June 28. The remaining 49 percent of Sugarloaf was acquired by Otten on August 30.

How quickly our ski world changed. Remember, Otten had purchased tiny Sunday River from the Killington group in 1980.

For the next 14 years, he had embarked on a development strategy that took Sunday River from 40,000 skier visits to some 500,000, either No. 2 in the Northeast in volume or effectively tied with Mount Snow for that title. His formula was remarkably simple. First, build attractively priced resort condos and fill those new beds to drive skier visits. Second, provide a snow surface on the mountain that was consistently better that the competition in the East. And third, reinvest the cash in expanded terrain, lifts, and mountain facilities, creating a story of newness and growth that would set Sunday River apart.

The late 1980s and early 1990s were not a time of rapid growth in terms of the size of the skier market or its participation rates. Sunday River's growth came at the expense of the competition. Most of the pain was felt in New Hampshire and Maine, as Sunday River drew the majority of its clientele from the Boston market. But that was changing as the resort broadened its appeal, with Vermont and New Hampshire operators now looking nervously at their energized competitor. The Killington management team, having once owned the resort, was particularly sensitive. Let's just say numerous public barbs were traded over the years.

Les was well-aware of one of the old maxims for success: change the rules because they're stacked against you. In terms of public relations, he was a bit of a Donald Trump, recognizing the value of any publicity, whether good or bad. He had a knack for positioning himself on the front page ... often with his image-building golden retriever at his side. Sunday River's marketing was aggressive and bold, and based on the clever use of adjectives. The resort's signature White Heat trail wasn't the steepest in New England, but it was the "longest steepest widest" (with no commas). Les understood the power of "-est."

On the real-estate front, he built functional, inexpensive condos, and then more of the same. This at a time when most of the industry was competing to provide a higher-quality (and more expensive) resort experience to compete with what was happening out West. You didn't think "master-planned community" when you visited Sunday River.

But the planning was appropriate to the quality of the lodging. And virtually every unit had ski-trail access. Customers didn't seem to care. The competition groaned. He built a 200-room hotel, the Sunday River Grand Summit, using framed construction. It sold in quarter-shares, making it essentially a time-share product and guaranteeing occupancy. You could sit in your room and listen through near-paper-thin walls to people walking down the hallway. Again, the buyers and guests generally didn't care. They were not looking for a Deer Valley experience. The price was right, the amenities satisfactory, and the hotel slopeside. It sold so quickly that he added another wing, bringing it to more than 300 rooms. Between 1983 and 1997, he reportedly sold 1,350 condominiums at Sunday River alone.

This obvious success in real-estate development could not have occurred if he hadn't established a competitive advantage in his on-mountain skiing product. Providing a consistent, quality snow surface in New England is an immense engineering and operating challenge. Snowmaking is required on virtually all terrain, given the inevitable thaw-and-rain cycles that occur even in "good" natural-snow years. These cycles are aggravated by notoriously high humidity. It's as if nature was continually trying to turn snow crystals into water . . . frozen water.

Les was arguably the first in New England to understand that machine-made snow had to be as dry as possible in order to deal with these weather cycles and high humidity. Drier snow allowed liquid precipitation to "drain" through it, avoiding the usual transformation into frozen granular, the nemesis of Eastern skiers. He embraced a technology called "high-pressure air," which has since been discarded as snowmaking science evolved. But at the time, the combination of well-trained snowmakers, "high-pressure" air, and homemade-snow guns worked miracles, along with allowing the machine-made snow to "cure" for a day or two before grooming.

The drier snow was laid down on redesigned or new trails that were indeed wider and steeper than most of the Eastern resorts provided at the time. I remember my first visit in the late 1980s with my family . . . a midwinter getaway, a busman's holiday, if you will. While the experience off-mountain was minimalist, we were there to ski, and we were blown away. If you were an experienced blue- or black-run skier, Sunday River was providing the best snow surface in the Northeast. Hands down. It was also really steep! Obviously, the steeper the terrain, the more important snow quality is. And Sunday River had it.

DURING THOSE YEARS, Les built a large, dedicated year-round staff. Virtually all on-mountain folks would shift to construction projects in the spring, their labor "capitalized" for the non-skiing portion of the year. He was aggressive in employing this accounting strategy, driving EBITDA as well as providing jobs. That said, the quality of construction no doubt suffered over what would have been provided by using more independent contractors.

In acknowledging Sunday River's successes, Otten's emphasis on ski school needs to be included. He recognized that stealing market share could only go so far. The long-term health of his company and the ski industry would depend on increasing the number of participants. He put considerable energy into developing what he called the "Perfect Turn Ski School." Cornerstone for the program was the new "shaped ski," originally with Elan, then Rossignol, which allowed ski instructors to progress students toward the carved turn in an accelerated manner. As the program evolved through time, most of Otten's resorts would feature Learning Centers with state-of-the-art video classrooms, rental shops, and pleasant greeting areas. For a period of time, Jonny Moseley, the well-known freestyle Olympic gold medalist, was his spokesperson. While other resorts were also focusing on reengineering the "learn-to" process, Otten was in the vanguard.

IN THE DAYS BEFORE HIS ACQUISITION OF S-K-I, I actually enjoyed a very positive working relationship with Les. He kept in regular contact with most of the Killington managers, especially CFO Marty Wilson, who was his mentor in the early Killington years (Wilson eventually served on the American Skiing Company board) and Foster Chandler. Les and I spoke by telephone late on Saturdays, during ski season, comparing notes on conditions, crowd volume, etc. He was obsessed with gathering intelligence, always wanting to know what was happening in Vermont. He was always good for a new joke, something I appreciated at the end of a long day.

While I made several midwinter trips to Sunday River to keep track of his innovations, I don't believe I accepted the reality that he was a legitimate competitor until shortly before his purchase of S-K-I. Given his distance from the markets (other than Boston) and lack of resort infrastructure, few in our company or, frankly, the entire Eastern ski establishment gave him enough credit or developed an appropriate competitive response. In hindsight, we were more than slow in addressing the snow-quality issue, something that had long been a Killington/S-K-I strength. Remember where Les came from.

Not content with his Sunday River success, Les went on a buying binge in

New England, a region where he understood the weather and the markets. In July 1994 he acquired Attitash, New Hampshire. While Attitash was only a midsized New England ski area, it did compete with Sunday River and enjoyed a killer location in North Conway, where hundreds of thousands of tourists trekked annually to visit Mount Washington and enjoy the community's popular outlet shopping. Attitash was well-positioned to take advantage of this nonwinter traffic, and enjoyed a vigorous summer business. Being just a short drive to Sunday River, it was a logical first move for Les.

The president of Attitash at the time was Phil Gravink, former president of Loon Mountain and a longtime force in New England skiing. Those watching from the sidelines felt that the Gravink/Otten combination, while potentially strained, could bring some maturity and sound counsel to Les' growing organization. Phil was highly respected within the North Conway community and proved very effective in securing the development permits needed for Les' rapid expansion.

In October of that year, Otten purchased Sugarbush in the Mad River Valley of Vermont. Sugarbush had seen some five different owners since the early days of Damon Gadd and Jack Murphy, a 10th Mountain Division veteran. A young Blaise Carrig started there in 1976 as a patroller, advancing through the ranks to the role of general manager when Les bought the resort. Les brought in Allen Wilson, the former Killington controller and Bear Mountain finance VP, as company president. Blaise remained as VP and GM. Wilson eventually went on to Killington, post-Otten, as president, and Carrig headed off to the The Canyons to lead that project for Les. (Blaise would eventually rise to the role of president of the mountain division for Vail Resorts until his retirement in 2015.)

During the summer of 1995, Les acquired Cranmore Mountain, North Conway's iconic downtown ski hill. Les was making things happen, and many veterans in the business wanted to join him at that time. Me included.

THE APPLE OF LES' EYE WAS KILLINGTON. He was well-aware that the company's board was looking at "strategic alternatives." His offer was essentially a preemptive strike, taking away the chance that the sale of S-K-I would have gone through a more traditional, public-sale process. While from the outside, S-K-I seemed to be on its own track for success, not all was well in the home office.

The Bear Mountain investment had been driven by Pres. He saw an

underserved Southern California market and felt that with appropriate investments in snowmaking, Bear could be an immediate success. While there was
never any doubt over the size of the skier market, doing business in California
turned out to be much more complicated and expensive than anticipated. The
year of 1995 had also seen the replacement of the old, three-stage, 3.5-mile-
long Killington Gondola with the "Skyeship"—at significant cost. The original
lift had provided an access alternative to the 5-mile long Killington Road. It
also provided summer sightseeing revenue thanks to its location on Route 4,
Vermont's east-west highway. While the alternate access is important even to
this day, the skiing terrain was simply not popular. A couple novice routes took
skiers on a long and winding journey, one that wasn't often repeated. So the
replacement lift was essentially a transportation lift.

BUT PRES WENT OVER THE TOP WITH IT. His girlfriend led a design project
to give each cabin a unique exterior wrap. PR materials referred to the "art
gallery in the sky." The results were spectacular, but expensive. Cabins were
heated and included piped-in music, both of which, as I recollect, seldom
worked. There were several VIP cabins (available for reservation) with carpeting, plush bucket seats and drink holders. Good idea but absent a market. The
lift was spectacular, but in terms of driving visitation or improving utilization
of the gondola trail network, it was close to a bust. There were numerous trail
changes in the vicinity of Skye Peak, where the lift terminated, but all in, it
was an investment that didn't pencil.

Pres had also stepped back from day-to-day involvement. In 1994, Hank
Lunde had been promoted to president, while Pres maintained the CEO role.
The company had moved its corporate offices from Killington to West
Lebanon, New Hampshire. The 1995 Annual Report noted: "We announced
in February that the company had received expressions of interest from certain
outside parties concerning a potential merger with or acquisition of S-K-I and
that we had retained a financial advisor in connection with the evaluation of
those expressions of interest." No one was surprised that the company was sold
in 1996. That it was sold to Les Otten was a surprise to virtually all and a
shock to many.

With the acquisition of S-K-I, there were questions about potential market
dominance in the East, given that the purchase now put eight New England
resorts under Otten's control. Pursuant to a consent decree with the U.S.

Department of Justice in connection with the acquisition, Otten's company sold the assets of Cranmore and Waterville Valley for $17.2 million on November 27, 1996. While most observers understood that the Vermont resorts (Mount Snow, Killington, and Sugarbush) under one ownership might have raised eyebrows, it was hard to see the logic in requiring Otten to dispose of Waterville and Cranmore, both relatively small operations. At any rate, that's what happened, and he moved on.

Having cut his ski industry teeth at Killington, Les Otten had some very specific ideas on how it might be improved. In terms of senior management, Hank Lunde stepped down. There was no love lost between Hank and Les, so staying on was never an option. Hank was well-compensated for his efforts in preparing the company for a sale. But I do think it was bittersweet for him. He had made significant progress in resolving ongoing environmental issues with the State of Vermont (especially water and the potential Pico/Killington interconnect) and looked forward to seeing a base village finally begin to rise. He spent several years on the sidelines, and then was recruited as CEO for Mount Mansfield Co., leading the renaissance of Stowe for almost a decade before retiring in December 2008. Virtually all other members of the senior Killington team moved on quickly or assumed different roles. Leo Denis remained on in a part-time capacity doing risk management. Marty Wilson retired but eventually joined Les on the ASC board of directors. Dave Wilcox headed off to Okemo. Foster Chandler remained on in a consulting role for a few years. After I'd spent two years at S-K-I in business development and then as president of the Vermont areas, Les wanted me back at Mount Snow and not arguing with him about what should or should not happen at Killington. So back I went. Not happy, but understanding the rationale.

Les brought former Killington controller and Sugarbush President Allen Wilson in as Killington's president. Another Killington veteran, Tom Richardson (former controller), was on the LBO team as its CFO. "Fixing" Killington was going to be Les Otten's primary focus. As he often remarked to members of the old regime: "There isn't time to debate what we're going to do. I know what needs to be done, and I'm going to do it."

One of the frequently heard complaints about Killington was the number of confusing trail intersections and crossings. This was the result of a commitment to provide a novice route from each mountain area. Given Killington's traditionally huge learn-to-ski contingent, this trail plan was consistent with the goal of growing participation. Graduates of the learn-to-ski programs could explore the entire resort, knowing that there was always an easier way down. As time passed, however, fewer customers were beginners or novices, and more were advanced skiers looking for more consistent, fall-line skiing, so these crossings made less sense. During the summer of 1996, most were eliminated.

And Otten spent money, reinvesting in new facilities at all his acquired resorts, but nowhere more than at Killington. In 1997, a second gondola was constructed from the Killington parking lot (just west of the base lodge) to the summit of Killington Peak. Nearly every aspect of mountain operations was improved, but the base buildings remained largely in 1970s sameness, overcrowded, plainly designed, and, almost without exception, serving poor food. I think most Killington skiers would agree that, despite the Otten investments, a disconnect remained between the mountain and base-area experiences.

There's an argument that says Otten wanted to reposition Sunday River as the new Killington, given its scale, learn-to-ski emphasis, etc. There were any number of trail names at Sunday River that were just taken from the Killington map. If that was his strategy, what then was Killington? To Foster Chandler's point, "People will buy what you sell."

Well, Otten's ownership began a period where the public, and employees, didn't really know what Killington was anymore—and the marketers didn't know "what to sell." Eventually, it was marketed as the "Beast of the East." It's arguable that this shift ensured a steady decline of overall market share to resorts like Stowe, Okemo, and Stratton, which were all offering a more family-friendly environment. As one looks at the Eastern ski industry from the perspective of 2016, no major resort has lost more market share than Killington. Period. Was this all because of Les Otten? No. But it can be argued that he had a moment when the resort might have been successfully repositioned—and it didn't happen. At one point, it was estimated that Killington's volume had dropped by 50 percent. Those numbers are moving in a positive direction again, thanks, I'm told, to an improved skier experience. But the lack of new beds will diminish the upside.

One person who developed an informed perspective on the ASC/Killington transition was Larry Jensen, who joined the S-K-I team in the late '70s. I met Larry shortly after moving to Mount Snow in 1977. He was working as editor of the *Deerfield Valley News*, owned by a former real-estate salesman, actor, and all-around renaissance man, Don Albano. Larry and Don were very bright guys

and hugely overqualified for their small paper. They had made the decision to
raise their families in Vermont, and so be it. Larry was an exceptional writer
with an interest in the ski business, and I knew Pres Smith was looking for that
kind of talent. So Larry moved north to work for Pres, eventually acquiring his
MBA and becoming a senior-finance executive with the company.

After the sale to ASC, he moved on to become CFO for the Rutland Regional Medical Center. In 2007, *Skiing Heritage* journal published an article
on Les Otten ("When Les was More"), and Larry, feeling that there were a
number of misrepresentations, penned a letter to the editor noting his objec-
tions. The letter closes:

> "When Otten bought S-K-I, most of the team that Smith had
> assembled was still with the company. Many were immediately
> let go or left on their own. The rest were gone within two years.
> In the end, Otten failed his employees and investors completely.
> The sad thing is that Otten will never recognize or accept that
> his personal flaws were the seeds of this monumental failure."

But back to the bigger picture. The speed with which Les Otten assembled
and grew the American Skiing Company from 1996 to 1998 was simply stunning. The S-K-I purchase was followed quickly by Pico Mountain in October
1997. Killington and Pico had been vetting the potential for an interconnect
and, while not approved, Otten must have had confidence enough in the opportunity to move forward with the purchase.

In July 1997, Wolf Mountain, formerly known as Park West, was added
to the resort collection. It was promptly renamed The Canyons. This would
be Les Otten's first venture out West. While much of the property was transferred subject to expensive leases, the development rights or other interests
covered more than 7,100 acres, including sufficient land for an entirely new
base village. To my knowledge, there was no comparable ski-resort real-estate
development opportunity in the nation.

Excitement over the sales opportunity was also driven by the upcoming
Salt Lake 2002 Olympics, an event that would showcase Utah and The
Canyons to an international market. As a measure of their success in leveraging
the Olympics, The Canyons management team hosted the "Today" show from
its Grand Summit Hotel throughout the competitions. On the mountain, the
amount of potential skiable terrain was enough to dwarf the existing and then

much larger (by skier visits) Park City Resort. In fact, under Vail Resorts' current ownership, the two were connected in time for the 2015–16 ski season, making the combined resort, now simply Park City, the nation's largest. Certainly, Otten saw the opportunity.

On November 12, 1997, Steamboat in Colorado and Heavenly in Lake Tahoe were added to the ASC lineup for a price tag of some $290 million. That included a Florida golf course, Sabal Point, which was subsequently sold.

So where did the money come from? Various debt instruments had been used up until the Steamboat/Heavenly deal. Les controlled (with the banks) virtually the entire enterprise. To pull off the latest acquisitions required a major public offering that November, and so the American Skiing Company was formed. The funds from that offering brought in the cash to complete the acquisition, but left Otten with 51 percent of the business. It was successfully underwritten and the stock began trading on the New York Stock Exchange.

At the time, Les Otten was probably worth, on paper, some $500 million. In addition to the paper wealth, Les and senior executives were awarded "fully vested options to purchase 622,038 shares of the common stock at an exercise price of $2.00 a share" (per the June 11, 1997, prospectus). This resulted in a "one-time compensation charge of approximately $11.4 million in the first quarter of fiscal 1998," again, per the prospectus. The value of the public stock began its inexorable decline to near "worthless," but to the extent that the executives sold early on, all were well-compensated for their efforts in putting together the incredible 1996–98 run.

The 1998 Annual Report for ASC took pride in the recent accomplishments, and looked forward optimistically to the future. Here's what Chairman Otten wrote in his Letter to Shareholders:

> Fiscal 1998 was a year of outstanding accomplishment for American Skiing Company. We established the Company as the largest ski resort operator and developer in the nation. We doubled in size for the second time in as many years, with premier resorts now located in every major skiing market in the United States. We achieved record financial results across all key performance metrics, especially in our real-estate development program, which soared to new heights on a national basis.

ASC resorts accounted for almost 5 million skier visits, or 9.4 percent of the total skier visits in the U.S. for the 1996–97 season. These numbers were impressive. Equally impressive was the fact that these nine resorts gave ASC a presence in most major U.S. skiing markets. And each enjoyed significant appeal in those markets, whether regional or destination.

So how could things go wrong? Great resorts. Some 7,000 acres of developable real estate. Access to capital markets. Sponsor partners eager to join with the growing company.

While hindsight provides greater accuracy, most of the issues that led to the eventual downfall of ASC were evident in 1998. Others involved or observing the company may have a different view, but from my perspective the key contributors to failure were:

- The Chairman himself.

- Overly aggressive or ineffective capital investment in the existing and acquired resorts.

- A flawed real-estate strategy in its reliance on multiple Grand Summit hotels.

CHAPTER 4

Rise and Fall:

The Chairman's Role in the Debacle

A SC was very much Les Otten's company. He held 51 percent of the stock. His executive team was, at least initially, comprised of old friends and managers from Sunday River or Killington. Chris Brink led marketing. Burt Mills, his longtime mountain manager, had a hand in all major mountain capital decisions. Skip King, his longtime PR guru, led communications. Chris Howard, his Portland, Maine-based attorney, became in-house counsel. Tom Richardson, a former Killington controller, became CFO, although he stepped down from that role suddenly in August 1998, ostensibly for reporting-accuracy issues, and took the reins at Sugarbush. Warren Cook, former president of Sugarloaf, became COO in July 1998.

While all were capable, seasoned ski-resort professionals, they generally shared one view of how the ski world worked and that was Les' view. This was a team that had participated in and benefited from Otten's success. Cook was something of an exception in that he had been a longtime competitor, and joined the ASC leadership team only after Otten acquired S-K-I. Sometime in the mid '90s he had a sign installed on a lift tower halfway up one of Sugarloaf's main chairlifts that read, more or less: "If you were at Sunday River, you'd be at the summit now." Sugarloafers were typically disdainful of Sunday

River, feeling theirs was the real, "big" mountain. This sign infuriated Les, so when Otten bought S-K-I, Warren delivered the sign to Les, attached to a ball and chain. Such was his peace offering or job application, depending on your point of view.

This executive team was not a group that would challenge Otten's decision making. I remember sitting in the audience at a group meeting of ASC folks at the 1996 Charleston NSAA Convention when Burt Mills stated plainly: "Our job is not to provide input or debate decisions. It's to execute Les' vision." OK. Guess that's how things work around here.

LES HAD MANY STRENGTHS: superb mastery of the complexities of Eastern snowmaking, charismatic personality, tenacity, raw intelligence, marketing/salesmanship, and a true passion for the sport. He was masterful at generating personal publicity and careful to cement his public image: athlete, passionate skier, golden retriever at this side. He was also an exceptional communicator when on-stage. He seldom used notes, no matter how long the presentation. Those speeches could be mesmerizing for the audience. Les was well-aware that this was a strength, and seldom let others speak for ASC. That was his role, and he leveraged it well.

Until the Steamboat acquisition.

Steamboat and Heavenly had been owned by Kamori International Corporation, a Japanese company with ski-resort holdings in Japan. Kamori was reportedly very sensitive to any perception that, as international owners, they were overly involved with the day-to-day operation of the resorts. This led to a style of "benevolent ownership" that provided local management teams with considerable flexibility in how financial results were delivered. Ownership worked with local executives to develop an annual operating and capital plan and then let the managers execute. In my view, budgets were not overly aggressive, and as a result, there was a high degree of contentment with the Kamori ownership on the part of staff.

The acquisition closed in November 1997, too late in the year for any major capital investments or operating changes on the part of ASC. So for the most part, life continued as usual for employees.

That season also turned out to be one of bountiful snowfall, so ASC was probably satisfied that its plan was on track. Most of the attention of ASC executives was focused on getting the Steamboat Grand Summit through the permit process and into construction. The ASC real-estate team set up shop quickly and began selling quarter-shares (this was an interval ownership product) as soon as possible. Early on, there was considerable enthusiasm for the project. While some locals were dismayed by the scale (300-plus rooms, a tenth-of-a-mile long, with a second phase yet to come), there was general consensus that Steamboat needed new beds and a reinvigorated base area in order to compete. While the mountain facilities were attractive enough to consistently drive 1 million skier visits, the base area significantly detracted from the overall experience.

ASC presented new master plans for the base area and began a focused selling effort. There was significant interest by locals and second-home owners familiar with Steamboat. Certainly, these potential buyers were looking at Otten's success elsewhere and probably wanted a piece of the action.

Major capital spending in the summer of 1998 also drove early support for ASC. Snowmaking was extended to the summit of Storm Peak and numerous enhancements were made to the snowmaking infrastructure, giving Steamboat, for the first time, an opportunity to provide significant acreage and a good variety of terrain for early-season skiing.

It had been a long time since any major terrain expansion had occurred. The Kamori ownership was very conservative when it came to capital expenses, so while the resort performed necessary major maintenance, virtually no expansion projects had been undertaken in years.

The summer of 1998 saw extensive trail and lift work in the terrain north of the Storm Peak Lift. The new area was called Pioneer Ridge and opened for the 1998–99 season. At that time, the U.S. Forest Service (whose approval as landowner was needed for the project) had a "light on the land" philosophy in terms of projects like Pioneer Ridge. That meant virtually no significant earthwork. Since the project did not include snowmaking, Pioneer Ridge would need a significant amount of natural snow to open. The lift was a detachable quad, but was approved for only 1,200 passengers per hour, one-half of the design capacity. This was a big investment that made a statement about where Steamboat was headed, but it would need a good snow year to be well-utilized. When looking at the comfortable capacity of the mountain, Pioneer Ridge certainly increased that number, but only modestly.

The 1998–99 winter got off to a slow start as warm, dry weather settled in over the West. Coming out of the Christmas holiday period and looking at where ASC stood financially, it's fair to say that some level of panic set in. The company was highly leveraged with expensive debt. It needed to make the best of the challenging weather situation. I was at Mount Snow at the time, and back East we were used to challenging weather and the need to make quick changes of direction. Otten was a master at creating a sense of urgency. Although I wasn't in Steamboat at the time, I'm sure that he exhorted the local team to adjust course.

Steamboat's management had never experienced anything like Otten's intensity. Nor had they ever faced a cost-cutting situation like this under prior ownership, so they struggled with how to respond. Otten's frustration peaked in mid-January, and he discharged its president, Gary Mielke. Gary had been CFO before stepping into the top role. He had been in finance for several years, chaired the NSAA Economic Study Committee, and was well-respected inside and outside the organization.

Shortly after Gary's departure, the Steamboat management team settled on a cost-reduction plan per Otten's direction. The end result was the termination of some 15 longtime employees, most in management positions. While this was "voluntary" in the sense that each was offered a severance package, that was not the perception. The aftermath: the company and the community went into something close to a state of shock. The response to Otten was a prompt firestorm of animosity. The honeymoon was over.

EVEN WITHOUT THE REDUCTION IN FORCE, some very hard feelings had been developing between ASC and the Steamboat employees. Les wanted to brand all his ski schools under the "Perfect Turn" umbrella. This was a disaster in Steamboat. Longtime instructors with 20 to 30 years of experience felt as though they were being treated like children. They pushed back.

Burt Mills had been the driving force behind the extension of snowmaking to the top of Storm Peak. This was a very positive change and well-designed. But when Burt arrived to teach the mountain staff how to make snow the "Sunday River way," it was not well-received. There were fundamental differences between making snow back East and in the arid West. And Les and his team just wouldn't listen. ASC said "No Snomax" (a snowmaking additive) in order to save costs. He insisted on using small particle guns (Sunday River style). These were bad decisions and negatively affected the overall performance of the snowmaking department, so they too pushed back, despite recognition that the expanded snowmaking had been a very positive change.

In terms of IT and financial management systems, the ASC corporate infrastructure simply wasn't up to the task of efficiently absorbing the Kamori acquisition. Upgrades were made to the CODA accounting system without testing. The system crashed. Corporate marketing rolled out multiple-resort products like the "Magnificent 7" (good for seven days at any ASC resort) without appropriate testing. The system couldn't consistently track usage so savvy guests just kept using the pass product beyond seven days. Revenue recognition was a joke. That said, products like the "7" and the "Edge" card were industry breakthroughs. Some 20 years later, they are ubiquitous. Otten had the vision and foresight, but my view is that no one on his team would admit to him that they could not execute. Their technology simply wasn't up to the task.

Despite past successes, ASC also began to fail in terms of basic business execution. Steamboat staff was told that ASC would order snowmobiles. The ball was dropped and that came back onto the resort's lap late in the year. Same thing happened with other capital orders like magic carpet lifts. ASC's coordinated purchasing of uniforms was another disappointment for the resorts. The list of failures went on and on and on.

This was a clash of cultures if there ever was one. Steamboat's brand was built on its Western, family-friendly ranching culture. Add in champagne powder, real town and real people ... and that pretty well summed up how the community viewed itself. The employees were not prepared for Les when he showed up for meetings with his new golden retriever puppy that contributed liquid and solid deposits on the office-building carpets. The company had clear rules prohibiting pets from the workplace, but Les paid no heed. He was oblivious to how he was viewed and how the reaction was building. While completing the January workforce reduction, he flew in on the corporate jet. These things were noted.

Sherry Gibson, longtime employee and administrative assistant to Gary Mielke, remarked to me: "I knew one day how different things were going to be when I walked by the Headwall Meeting Room. The door was closed. Les and his real-estate people were inside screaming at each other. They used language that had never been heard in our building."

While these behaviors were on exhibition daily, the company was posturing itself as a service-driven organization. From the 1998 Annual Report: "In executing each of these initiatives, we strive to engage our guests in unique and memorable resort experiences inherently personal to each guest . . ." An organization cannot deliver world-class service to its guests unless it treats its employees and stakeholders the same way. A disconnect will, as it did, eventually take a toll in terms of the guest experience.

AS THE STEAMBOAT GRAND SUMMIT was coming out of the ground that winter of 1999, it became apparent to the ASC real-estate team that there were pricing issues relative to presales. Assumptions regarding the projected building costs had been too optimistic, and the pricing needed a total overhaul. There were three real-estate executives with key roles on the project: Mike Meyers oversaw construction, Greg Spearn was responsible for permitting, and Scott Oldakowski was the sales guy. Each had goals or targets that would determine their bonuses, but there seemed to be no genuine, collaborative effort to make sure that the entire project was a success. So there was constant bickering.

In order to right the ship, pricing needed a major overhaul and some additional "value engineering" had to occur. The last-minute cost cutting came out of finishing details, which affected the overall quality of the finished product. In addition, they decided to convey the hotel's garage to the HOA, saddling buyers with the obligation for a $6 million note and saving ASC that amount on the building cost. Other issues had been cropping up around the Grand, but the garage, as I recollect, became a very public spat and resulted in the cancellation of many of the presale agreements. Bottom line: the goodwill that was reflected in the early buy-in by locals (in terms of presales) was evaporating. Marketing materials promoting the Grand were evident throughout the Steamboat property, including the gondola cabins. Guests began defacing the "Grand Summit" banners buy adding an "l." Everywhere there were "Grand Summit" stickers, they became "Grand Slummit" stickers. Guess what? Sales slowed.

Bumper stickers began appearing on vehicles throughout town: "More Boat, Less Otten." Letters to the editor critical of ASC began to populate the local media. One of the more popular staff members let go in the job cutting was Pete Wither, the ski patrol director. The Wither family members were early settlers and Steamboat icons. So ads began appearing in the local paper with Pete's picture and the caption: "For Pete's Sake?" Unhappiness within the ski patrol was such that following the 1998–99 ski season, the patrollers voted to unionize. The ski patrol union remains in existence to this date, a sorry reminder of the divisiveness created during the Otten reign.

At one of his many public presentations, Les had made the comment that the Steamboat experience needed to be more like that of Beaver Creek or Deer Valley. I'm sure he was referring to the need for base-area upgrades, but the comments were taken out of context and confirmed to locals that he was taking Steamboat to a place where they absolutely did not want to go. This was a ski community comfortable in its skin. It was OK to update the base area, but no one was interested in changing the brand to be more like anybody. This simply scared people. It wasn't how they saw themselves, and, I think, many realized that it would be a failed strategy, causing everyone heartache and, eventually, financial loss.

I KNOW ALL THIS because I wound up right in the middle of it. I was busy at Mount Snow that winter getting the new Mount Snow Grand Summit open and completing a host of capital projects as a result of ASC's ownership. News of the troubles in Steamboat was now getting national attention, and I was aware of Mielke's departure. This was not a happy time for me, either. While it was satisfying to finally have some resources to take Mount Snow to a new level, I was experiencing the same cultural challenges as the Steamboat folks, just not with the intensity. The ASC culture was noncollaborative, just so different from S-K-I, even with its faults toward the end. My family knew that things weren't going well, and I was looking to move on, even thinking about getting out of the ski business.

Steamboat had been one of my favorite resorts since skiing there with then-president Hans Geier in the 1980s. Les asked if I would be interested in the Steamboat job. Fortunately, despite my discontent, I said "yes," and was flown out to see for myself what was going on. This was late January. It was my first and last trip in the corporate jet (it was sold or lease-terminated during the financial crisis that was to follow). Otten had a car at the Hayden airport where we landed. We raced off to Steamboat, with Otten driving so fast that he failed to negotiate the first sharp left-hand turn as we left the airport. Fortunately, the car just slid to a stop in a snowbank. We successfully extricated ourselves and headed to town. I always thought of that moment as a metaphor for the entire ASC experience: Otten going at breakneck speed, crashing, and then moving on as if nothing had happened.

My visit to Steamboat told me that the crisis level in terms of staff and community relations could be managed, if Otten would just stay away for a while. He was the touchstone. We just needed time to sort things out and regain credibility. He basically agreed and, to his credit, stepped off center stage. In terms of the ASC cultural issues, I wasn't so naive as to think I could make those go away. But I did feel that the current ASC path was not sustainable. Cultural changes would have to occur or Otten would soon be gone.

Unfortunately but understandably, I was perceived in the community as Les Otten's "lackey," and a fair amount of animosity was directed toward me for some time. Since my kids were both attending Wilmington High School in Vermont, I had made the move to Steamboat by myself in February. I would head home for a weekend when possible, and the family came out several times that winter so we didn't become total strangers.

The company rented an apartment for me and, as I look back, it was fortunate that I was alone. First, there was so much to be done in terms of understanding, and then repairing, relationships. This meant long days and nights attending public meetings. Second, my family didn't have to experience the animosity when it was at its height. (As evidence of how slowly it dissolved, when my wife and daughter went to meet the assistant principal at Steamboat High School to talk about her attendance the following fall, his opening salvo was, "So, you're the family everyone hates." Not surprisingly, Elizabeth decided to attend Lowell Whiteman, the local private school).

Here's another memory I can laugh about now: getting my post office box at our downtown post office (there was no rural delivery to my condo). There was a line at the post office (I soon learned there's always a line). I heard the whispering from behind the counter: "That's the guy." I stood there sheepishly for about 5 minutes as the line slowly moved. It seemed like everyone was staring at me, especially an older gentleman standing behind the counter . . . clearly someone in charge. When I finally got to the counter and began filling out the box rental form, the clerk somewhat sarcastically asked: "Will that be 6 months or a year?" I responded: "One year. I'm an optimist."

I took my new key and headed off in search of the box. It wasn't as far away as you could be from the front desk . . . but close. It took me awhile to find it because it had a piece of tape where the decal would normally be. But there it was: 774763, faint but there.

I tried to open it with my key, but the key didn't work. Aaaargh. Back to the long line. The senior gentleman (who had been standing back) waved for me to come forward and asked what the problem was. I said very quietly:

"Sir, my key doesn't work."

"Follow me," he said.

So back to my new mailbox went the two of us, again with the crowd watching and murmuring. It took some time as he had to remove the old lock and replace it. This was done with some loud hammering and pounding, but not a word said between us. Lock repaired, he introduced himself as the postmaster. I later learned that his wife had recently parted ways with Ski Corp. I'm not sure if it was part of the Otten-ordered reduction or not. Small town. Hard feelings. I still have the same box: No. 774763.

One other anecdote worth reporting: Steamboat is notorious for its proliferation of nonprofits. Sometimes, I think there are more nonprofits than cows. One of the largest and most significant was and is the Yampa Valley Community Foundation. The Ski Corp. had a special relationship with the YVCF in that it generously provided ski passes, lockers, and parking privileges, which the foundation then sold to "Passport Club" members. These funds essentially covered the operating expenses of the nonprofit, just less than $200,000 at the time. I was invited to a social gathering of the club at a private residence in upscale Dakota Ridge. The place was packed, since attendees had been promised an update from the new Ski Corp. president. That I did, trying to be objective about the ASC financial challenges, but upbeat in terms of Steamboat's prospects. There were a number of questions and comments, most highly critical of ASC, as you might imagine. One woman went into a lengthy diatribe on the subject of the Steamboat Grand, how she thought it was too big, etc. "But what I really don't understand is how could the City planning people have approved that ugly yellow color for the exterior?"

I responded, as tactfully as possible, that the yellow was the color of the rigid insulation and would disappear once the exterior siding was applied. One of the guests, Jim Larson, who eventually became a close friend, broke out in a huge laugh. Well, I guess I'd made one convert. With that, the cocktail party was over. Thank goodness.

One final comment on the chairman's role in ASC's downfall. In late summer 1998, the ASC management teams were invited to a conference back in Maine. This was a large group. Each resort sent its resort chief plus mountain operations, marketing, and finance heads. Spouses were invited, although few went. The real-estate group and corporate folks were there as well, so all told the group totaled close to 100. This was presented as both a business meeting and a chance to relax. I was at Mount Snow at the time (just a four-plus hour drive), and Eileen accompanied me (it was our 20th wedding anniversary). She was one of a handful of spouses who attended. To this day she still hasn't forgiven me.

The location was a camp for boys that had probably been around for more than 50 years, located on a small lake near Sunday River. The campers had just left and ASC took over the property. Barely enough time for a tidying up, let alone a thorough clean. There were two kinds of lodging available: tents with wooden platforms or small bunkhouses. As I recollect, those with spouses got the bunks with a solid roof. Only one problem: someone had decided that it would be a nice touch to include a welcoming chocolate on each pillow. This was the equivalent of putting a sign in the hallway: "Attention Mice, Feed Zone Ahead." The rattle and scurry was incredible. No one could sleep. The stench of mouse droppings permeated the entire bunkhouse we were in. The platform tents didn't provide a much better experience. Gary Mielke and Rod Hanna, also from Steamboat, went to a local hardware store to buy plywood in an attempt to make their bunks "sleepable." Hanna checked into a local motel for night No. 2.

On the arrival day, Les was putting his ski boat in the water with plans for some waterskiing. The boat wouldn't start. He was not happy and sent his son to the dealership to buy a replacement, which arrived later that night.

Evening activities were centered around the main lodge, where food was prepared. The first night featured a Maine lobster dinner, after which a comedian entertained with very funny Maine jokes ... accent included. On night two, a second comedian showed up for after-dinner entertainment and told the exact same jokes. Ugh. The only other entertainment was poker ... games broke out each night. This was something that Les enjoyed very much.

We had meetings during the day, discussing a variety of resort issues, mostly led by COO Warren Cook. The real-estate people were expected to participate, but were almost never in the room. They could be seen on cell phones on the meeting room porches, conducting business ... oblivious to what the rest of the group was doing.

ASC was all Otten. The "off-site" at a boys' camp was his idea. His party. How it turned out said a lot about how the future would unfold ... right down to the same bad jokes told over and over.

CHAPTER 5

Money Well Spent?

The Spending Spree

From the Chairman's Letter in the 1998 Annual Report for the American Skiing Company:

> "Based on these impressive results, we will continue to fully im-
> plement our successful operating strategies across all resorts ac-
> quired during the past two years. This year's introduction of
> four hotels, five lodges, three learn-to-ski discovery centers, nine
> high-speed quads and two high-speed gondolas, together with
> a host of other attractions, will provide memorable guest expe-
> riences for years to come."

And from the 1999 Letter:

> "...In the past two years alone, we have invested more than
> $145 million in our multi-resort network."

So, how effectively were these dollars employed? Below are observations relative to some of the larger resort projects:

Sunday River

While Sunday River had been growing at a breakneck pace, the late '90s took even that to a new level. Otten added two new skiing areas, Oz Bowl and Jordan Bowl. The distance from the original, modest base area and ski complex to Jordan Bowl by car was now some 10 miles.

To reach Jordan on skis could take several hours, passing from one mountain area to another as if moving along a lengthy ridge line. While there was a sameness to much of the skiing, there was no question as to the challenge or snow quality. There were now eight mountain areas. But Jordan probably turned out to be the equivalent of a "Bridge Too Far." To anchor the Jordan end of the resort, Otten's plan called for a second Grand Summit, more real estate and a golf course about two miles away from the Jordan Base. This second base area had significant real-estate development potential. To provide access, he would need a long private road. The road construction, requiring huge cuts and fills, was done on-the-fly and on-the-cheap. It had to be entirely rebuilt under recent CNL ownership. The Jordan brand, given its remoteness, didn't sell at the pace of the original Grand Summit. I can't recollect the skier-visit trends at Sunday River over those late '90s years, but my sense is that they stabilized. Its primary markets were still Maine, southern New Hampshire, and eastern Massachusetts. Driving business from the wealthier enclaves of Connecticut and New York had proven difficult. So Sunday River had increased the cost of operations due to the Oz/Jordan expansion, but probably found itself ahead of the market instead of responding to demand. Jordan Bowl indeed became a "Bridge Too Far." Going forward, management would struggle with the need to connect all the mountains by Christmas (in order to keep Jordan Grand owners appeased). This reality put a cost structure in place that remains problematic to this day.

Attitash

Shortly after purchasing Attitash in 1994, Otten launched a major terrain expansion, developing a second mountain area and changing the name from Attitash to Attitash Bear Peak. This expansion almost doubled the skiing terrain, and provided a second base area with significantly expanded parking. A new Grand Summit Hotel was constructed at the base of Bear Peak and included many skier-service facilities, in addition to the normal Grand Summit features. An adventure park with a ropes course was constructed next to the hotel to assist in growing the corporate-meeting business by providing team-building exercises. The original Attitash base area was squeezed into a wedge of land between the main highway and slopes. Bear Peak by contrast had a large, flat assembly area at its base. It was an ideal location to develop group business.

The changes took Attitash from a modest local area to a more medium-sized venue, with plenty of New England charm and the capacity to handle considerable skier-visit growth. Had Otten's empire stopped at this point, Attitash would probably have moved to a stronger position in the market. But as the ASC collection grew, Attitash became something of an afterthought and, in my judgment, remained an unfinished painting. Add to that the recent resurgence of Loon Mountain and Bretton Woods, and its market share has probably been moving the wrong direction.

Sugarbush

Sugarbush was also acquired in 1994. The resort had for years struggled to maintain market share, mostly because of its challenging location on Vermont's narrow and winding Route 100, north of Killington and south of Stowe. A skier's choice was to pass by Killington (which traditionally offered more reliable snow) or turn south on Route 100 off Interstate 89 instead of travelling a short distance north to Stowe. It also suffered from an aging lift infrastructure, poor snowmaking, and a weak water supply. The base amenities were satisfactory, but certainly didn't provide a competitive advantage. It needed new beds. Sugarbush was actually two ski areas, the original Sugarbush resort and Mt. Ellen (which Otten renamed Sugarbush North). They were separated by a distance of some 3 miles. Mt. Ellen did not have a base village and was mostly skied by locals.

The one clear point of difference between these two mountains and the Killington facility was the length and continuous vertical drop offered by its trail complex. "South" included the legendary terrain of Castlerock, while many locals favored "North" for its pure fall-line skiing and ideal northern exposures. The runs were long and challenging and, unlike Killington, didn't require a lot of traversing. Otten determined that the best way to deal with broadening the appeal and increasing market share was to connect the two resorts with a long, detachable chairlift. How he managed to move this quickly through the permit process is credit to his tenacity (and that of his planning team). There was a real-estate component to the Slide Brook project, but it never got off the ground.

In addition to the new interconnect, other capital investments focused on improved snowmaking, plus new and reconfigured chairlifts. The makeover was marketed by ASC as a $25 million project, and billed as the largest one-year investment ever in a ski resort.

Sugarbush was now updated to the point where, other than access and new beds, it could stand up to the competition.

I'm quite sure that when Les acquired the resort, he expected to grow skier visits at the expense of first Killington and then Stowe. Had he not acquired Killington, that strategy might have worked. But by almost immediately re-calibrating the Killington skiing experience, he leveled the playing field against himself. Otten had grand plans for a base-area redevelopment, including a Sugarbush Grand Summit Hotel at South, but he underestimated the local resistance to a project of that size, and it was eventually scrapped. A real-estate revenue stream never developed to offset the on-mountain capital investments ... nor did the anticipated new beds that would drive skier visits. Bottom line: all the investment at Sugarbush merely maintained its market share, did not grow the business, and did not provide the expected return.

In fiscal 2001, the resort was sold to a group led by former Merrill Lynch executive Win Smith. ASC was desperate for cash at the time, and Smith's timing was perfect. ASC certainly never recovered its investments in Sugar-bush, as the 2003 Annual Report states: "This sale generated net proceeds of $5.2 million..." Further, the sale "resulted in an impairment charge of $15.1 million..."

Fast forward to 2016, and the interconnect lift is operated on peak days only, mostly weekends and holidays. Some nice new beds have been added in the slopeside Clay Brook lodge at South, but the scale of real-estate development has not been sufficient to drive incremental skier visits. Once again: location, location, location.

Killington

While Killington had an extensive snowmaking system, there were significant deferred costs in terms of old pipe, compressors, pumping facilities, and old, inefficient snow guns. ASC made notable improvements in updating the system and expanding it by some 30 percent. While Otten paid a premium to market valuation for S-K-I, the purchase looked downright cheap relative to subsequent transactions in ski country (premium destination resorts attracting valuations as high as 10 times EBITDA). That said, deferred capital expense at all the S-K-I resorts drove the total investment upwards. In the case of Killington, while the resort did receive a new Children's Center, the old Killington and Snowshed Lodges remained largely unchanged.

The three-year plan to connect Pico never happened. Despite interminable meetings and analysis, the Vermont permit process simply killed it by neglect. As a standalone, Pico was still a local hill, with little pricing strength. Even with consolidated management and group-buying to reduce costs, the Pico acquisition never penciled.

The Killington (K-1) Gondola certainly raised skier satisfaction in the Upper Basin area. Was it over the top? If the difference between the gondola and a detachable chairlift (probably some $5 million) had gone into improved base facilities, would the overall resort appeal have been greater?

Most importantly, while Otten continued the planning efforts needed to get a base village going, nothing happened beyond the construction of the Killington Grand Summit.

Mount Snow

Capital spending at Mount Snow following the acquisition was largely driven by the location selected for the Grand Summit Hotel. Pre-ASC planning efforts had always focused on the so-called Mixing Bowl Slope, with the idea that, with just a few structures, the old base-lodge area and Sundance Lodge could be connected. Also, day-skier guests could access the mountain facilities by walking through the new facilities from the lower parking areas. Pedestrian connections could be created along the ski edge, providing an extended "beachfront" for the ski area.

Instead, Otten decided to place the hotel on the large bench at the top of Mixing Bowl and the base of Beaver slope. This effectively cut the resort in half, required a long driveway from the lower lots to the hotel entrance, and called for shortening or relocation of several lifts. Lift 7 was split into two lifts ... a good idea, as it was too long as initially constructed. The Ego Alley Triple was shortened to make room for the hotel. One lift went away. The hotel was similar to other eastern Grand Summits: inexpensive wood-frame construction, utilitarian function space, basic décor in public areas and condominium interiors. Mount Snow's old base lodge was expanded to the south, creating a better connection to the new hotel and shortening the perceived walking distance.

Two significant changes were made to the lift system. High-speed quads were installed to replace older fixed-grip lifts, one at Carinthia and another on the old Standard trail, replacing two double chairs. These were the most appealing changes made to the ski mountain in many years.

Mount Snow's biggest need at the time was for additional water supplies for its snowmaking system. Little progress was made in that regard. It's interesting to note that after several decades of planning and permitting, a new and expanded reservoir system, expected to provide Mount Snow with additional water in time for the 2016–17 season, has now been delayed to 2017–18. As with Killington, with the exception of the new hotels, no progress was made relative to a larger base-area project.

Heavenly

The big story at Heavenly was the creation of a new gateway from downtown South Lake Tahoe. Years in the planning, a new gondola made the mountain connection from the busy casino area, in effect making the town "slopeside." ASC's vision called for a Grand Summit at the base of the gondola, but high-level discussions had been ongoing with Marriott time-share executives, with the idea that Marriott would build fractional properties at multiple ASC resorts. The Heavenly deal with Marriott did go forward (on the property identified for the Grand), but their experience was such that no other project was started with ASC. In fact, according to former ASC folks involved at the time, the Heavenly experience changed Marriott's view of the entire time-share world and led to a more conservative strategy on their part.

As outlined in ASC's 2001 restructuring plan, the Steamboat resort was to be sold. Heavenly turned out to be the "backup plan," and was sold to Vail Resorts. I suspect that many of the gondola-related investment costs wound up "stranded." Vail Resorts was happy. ASC survived . . . for the moment.

The Canyons

The spending in Utah proceeded at breakneck speed. In just a few years, ASC added five quads and a gondola, and dramatically expanded the skiing terrain. The resort aimed to put its best face forward in time for the 2002 Olympics, and it did, hosting the NBC "Today" show in the Canyons Grand, as noted. The dilemma for ASC was the lack of EBITDA flowing annually from The Canyons, given the high operating costs of the sprawling resort versus its current volume. There is always a period of imbalance along the growth curve. That it happened when ASC was experiencing a host of other issues only complicated the situation. Top-line revenues were not a problem. EBITDA was.

ASC sold The Canyons to Talisker in July 2007, and then closed its Park City offices. You all know what happened next, and we'll come back to that later.

Summary
ASC had acquired resorts with unprecedented speed over a two-year period. Until the public offering in 1997, the company had been piling up debt. The offering bought some time. Success in the ski business is always, to some degree, subject to the whims of Mother Nature. The 1998–99 season was a poor snow year in the markets ASC served. The fact that capital spending had been as aggressive, as noted above, left the company little wiggle room. Otten was spending to drive volume, and the volume didn't respond, given the weather or unrealistic expectations. A more conservative approach would have been to delay investments until annual EBITDA could catch up. But that was not the ASC way. The mantra: Be bold and aggressive. Les was a very good baseball player (and later, a part-owner of the Boston Red Sox). He didn't believe in bunts and singles. He swung for the fences.

And then there were problems on the real-estate side.

CHAPTER 6

Does One Size Fit All?

The Grand Summit Hotels

We all know about Les Otten's success with the original Sunday River Grand Summit Hotel. With a low cost of construction and virtually no land cost, the product could be priced attractively while still providing Sunday River with significant cash. The property was sold in quarter-shares, so unlike most time-shares, the buyer actually got a deed and was able to use the unit every fourth week. The condominiums ranged from studios to large penthouse units, and were ideal for buyers who lived within driving distance. Financing was readily available to qualified buyers. The marketing was what one might call "on-location saturation": everywhere you went on the resort property, there was a Grand Summit message.

If the sales team could lure potential buyers onto the property, there was a good chance of closing the deal. Nothing like this was being offered in New England at the time. The amenity package was very attractive: outdoor, heated pool; fitness area; several restaurants; large open lobby with fireplace; owner lockers; valet parking; and slopeside access. A key feature was the large locker area, where owners were assigned a locker for their family's skis, apparel, etc. Buyers could access their locker and enjoy the hotel's amenities even if it wasn't "their week." Another popular feature: owners could use the hotel on a "space available" (or Space A) basis, for a modest housekeeping charge. This drove occupancy, increasing revenue in the hotel's profit centers (F&B, retail, etc.), but, most importantly, helped to sell lift tickets. Most Sunday River skiers were predominantly weekend skiers, so this property was a great fit relative to their usage patterns. An owner could just come up for the day and enjoy the facilities without the hassle of schlepping ski equipment. An added perk to owners within the system would be the ability to travel to other ASC Grand Summits on a trade or Space A basis. Given the convenience of locker storage, Sunday River owners probably didn't spend much time skiing other areas . . . another competitive advantage the hotel provided.

To drive occupancy outside the ski season, the Grand Summit included expansive meeting space for conventions, and a large ballroom that could double as a trade-show facility.

In addition to the profits generated by a successful sell-through, the resort benefitted from increased skier visits and the revenues from the hotel's profit centers, the commercial space owned by the developer. These included restaurants, bars, retail, rental, etc.

The most important of these was the front desk. If owners chose not to use their week or weeks, they could provide Sunday River with the unit for sale to the general public. Sunday River was also the property manager, for which it received a fee. So the Grand Summit provided one-time cash from the sale of the quarter-shares, but also an ongoing stream of income from the operation of the facility. Because the resort owned the front desk, back offices, and reservation areas, there was no practical way for a competitor to bid for the profitable rental component of the business. Owners were effectively stuck with Sunday River or its designee as the manager. The hotel's sales office converted to "resales" once the property was fully subscribed, providing another valuable income stream.

If one hotel could be so successful, why not build 10 or 20? The pinnacle year for ASC was arguably 1998. From that year's Chairman's report, Les Otten comments: "We reached full stride in our real-estate development program by completing and delivering three 200-room Grand Summit Hotels at our New England resorts and commencing construction on three additional hotels at our Western properties."

My recollection is that the Eastern hotels came on line in roughly this order: first the Jordan Grand, then Attitash, then Killington, and, finally, Mount Snow.

While all were completed by 1998, the Eastern hotels were moving forward at different sales speeds. Killington, as might be expected, was the most successful in terms of sales. The Killington hotel was not slopeside (it was a short walk across a bridge to the Snowshed area), but it represented the first new lodging project in many years, and the amenity package was a good fit for the market. Attitash suffered somewhat from its location, slopeside but at the base of the newly expanded Bear Peak. Its remoteness and the overall weaker appeal of Attitash were a challenge for the sales team. At the end of July 2001, 40 percent of the units remained unsold. As a result, the company executed an auction strategy that engineered a complete sellout in fiscal 2002. The Mount Snow sales pace trailed Killington's, but was close to expectations.

Out West, The Canyons and Steamboat were under construction from roughly 1998 to 2000. As noted earlier, a project was being vetted for Heavenly in conjunction with the new gondola. The Canyons Grand Summit opened one year ahead of Steamboat, and was unquestionably the finest property built to date. A visitor to the "soft opening" in February 2000 arrived at midnight to find Blaise Carrig and Chip Carey, the resort president and marketing director, respectively, eating a very late dinner. Along with their entire management team, they had been working nonstop on finishing touches to open the property on time. After checking in, the visitor found a carpenter's tool belt left in the bathroom, and several fixtures, including the toilet paper dispenser, not yet installed.

While the property was finished in classic Otten hell-bent style, The Canyons Grand Summit was a huge success, with buyers lining up pre-construction to reserve a unit, and even camping overnight to hold their spot. Given proximity to the Salt Lake airport (a 30-minute drive) and the amount of air service from Southern California, the quarter-share model worked, especially for guests who preferred multiple, long weeks over the ski season.

Unlike the Eastern hotels, The Canyons project was concrete and steel, some seven floors in a U-shaped design right at the base of the rapidly expanding resort, where a new Cabriolet (open gondola) had been constructed to bring day skiers from remote parking areas to the resort base. Construction cranes were everywhere. Comparing The Canyons base to that of Park City was an eye-opener: one was new, and the other just looked old and tired. Food and beverage facilities were first class, and a talented culinary team made sure that the food quality matched the surroundings. Guests could walk out the slopeside entrance and, minutes later, climb aboard a new, eight-passenger gondola. Given the project's quality and the overall energy surrounding The Canyons' development, The Canyons Grand Summit sold well. But this was a huge project, over 300 rooms, and it would take several years for all the inventory to be absorbed, even given the hype surrounding the resort's growth. Enthusiasm for The Canyons was such that the next major condominium project, Sundial Lodge, sold out quickly.

But The Canyons' success was not being repeated elsewhere. As noted earlier, the Steamboat Grand saw many of its presales disappear, and once opened, the sales pace lagged well behind expectations.

So problems began to surface. While there was no arguing the success of the original Sunday River project, there were issues with the business model, particularly as it was moved west to a more discerning customer. First was the sheer size of the buildings, and the fact that they could not be constructed in phases. The promise made to buyers was that when the hotel opened, all amenities would be in place: locker room, fitness center, indoor/outdoor pool, meeting and conference space, owners' club, etc. The up-front costs for planning, permitting, marketing, and sales were significant, not to mention that some six hotels were coming online within a few years of each other. As long as everything was selling, the model worked. There were economies of scale in that the designs were very similar. Legal documents and HOA regulations could be duplicated, depending on differences in state laws. The marketing and sales efforts were centrally controlled, offering some savings. And ASC owned the land under each project.

With so many projects moving forward and with the size of the upfront cash commitments, there was little room for error, even following the successful public offering of 1997. The Steamboat Grand didn't help ASC's cash situation. One could argue that it was another "bridge too far."

Like other Grand Summits, it was built on land owned by the company. In order to provide financing separate from the resort debt, developable properties at Steamboat and elsewhere were transferred to American Skiing Company Resort Properties (ASCRP). The parcel selected for the Steamboat hotel was called "The Knoll." It had the advantage of being "vested" under city planning rules as a large hotel (the Courchevel) and had long been contemplated for the site. While it was not "slopeside," it was the closest parcel owned by ASCRP that could support a building of its size.

The biggest challenge the site offered was the need to have guests cross the busy Mount Werner Road to access the ski base area and gondola. Within the city planning staff, there were differing views on how the hotel should be integrated with the "old" base area, known as Gondola Square. Some believed that Mount Werner Road should terminate at Ski Time Square Drive (roughly across from the hotel's entry) and the existing parking structure across from the south end of the proposed hotel. Closing off the road was seen as a way to resolve the pedestrian-access issues and make the hotel more "connected," if not slopeside. This view was strongly enough held that the city required street-front retail to be constructed at grade along Mount Werner Road between the hotel entrance and its southern end, the area where the road would be abandoned.

There were several issues with this plan. First, the merchants in the Ski Time Square area (the original ski base area) recognized that this would impact the free flow of traffic and reduce visitation to their businesses. Most outspoken was Doug Terry, owner of Terry Sports, located in a commercial condominium in Torian Plaza, the slopeside component of the old Ski Time Square. Doug was effective at mustering opposition to any circulation changes and would complain that ASC had plans to move the road to the north side of the hotel and cut off access to Ski Time Square.

I was not in Steamboat at the time of the hotel's public project review, but got an earful when I arrived. My sense was that the ASC real-estate folks had been focused almost exclusively on getting the project permitted and under way and were not interested in waiting for the community to decide how to resolve circulation issues. The second problem with the road-closure idea was that of impracticality. Anyone observing the high volumes of traffic accessing the base area (including the transit center), would recognize that terminating Mount Werner Road at the hotel simply wasn't workable, given the volume of traffic. It might have proven workable if remote parking was enhanced and a new transportation lift system put in place. But there was little appetite and no money for such a plan. City Council couldn't make a decision one way or the other, nor did they did not want to hold up the "vested" project. There was still considerable goodwill relative to the new company and its plans to invest in the mountain and base area. While some complained about the size of the hotel or its design, few argued that the community wouldn't benefit from a second convention hotel (complementing the existing Sheraton Resort).

Given the desire to defer, Council established a Traffic Study Committee and charged that group with providing recommendations on parking and circulation. I served on that committee, and while it took a few years, we eventually came to a conclusion that upheld the status quo relative to circulation and agreed that the hotel's parking plan was adequate. Kudos to Chris Corna, former owner of the Slopeside Bar and Grill, who helped ensure civil discussions and effectively resolved the issues. It was a sad day for Steamboat when Chris died tragically in May 2009.

Unfortunately for the sale of quarter-shares at the Grand, there was a great deal of media coverage on the traffic and parking issue, much of it negative. How the property was viewed by the public was also affected by a glitch with a portion of the parking garage. One section of the garage, the north end, could not accept large SUVs with rooftop carriers. This is not unusual, given clearance issues in most parking structures. In fact, it was only one end of the garage that had a limitation. But the media had a field day, and the Grand's public image suffered.

Ironically, with the exception of the Torian Condominiums, virtually all of Ski Time Square was razed in 2009 in anticipation of redevelopment. That property had been owned by the same partnership that owned a majority of the Sheraton. Both were also sold shortly after Steamboat Ski & Resort Corp. was sold to Intrawest in 2007. Even though the amount of traffic headed into Ski Time Square is now greatly reduced from earlier days, consensus remains that leaving the road in place was the best solution. Unfortunately, that rang the death knell for street-level retail at the Grand (required by the City). There are a few funky shops and some offices, but generally, this remote cluster of retail spaces remains unoccupied.

I mentioned earlier that numerous presales to locals and vacation-home owners were cancelled in light of negative news. First was the pricing change based on underestimates of constructed cost and next was the garage note that became an obligation of the HOA. Finding good news about the Grand became harder and harder as time passed, especially as community hostility grew toward Les Otten personally.

It was difficult for Steamboat guests to miss seeing the bumper stickers, such as the one referring to the hotel as the "Grand Slummit" and proclaiming

"More Boat, Less Otten." (Another called the property the "Grand Sellout," and came with the message, "More for Les, Less for you.")

Dealing with the "Grand Slummit" sticker was easy. We changed the name to "The Steamboat Grand." Changing attitudes toward the hotel and ASC would take years.

CHAPTER 7

Welcome to Steamboat:
How Long Will You Be Staying?

I arrived in Steamboat in February of 1999, shortly after President Gary Mielke's firing and the departure of a dozen-plus mid-management veterans. In addition to dealing with the uproar relative to ASC, an immediate challenge was preparing to operate the hotel in December of that year, the advertised opening date, just 10 months away. Having a firm date was critical for several reasons: first, maintaining the credibility of the real-estate group to deliver an on-time project; second, meeting the expectations of buyers as to when they could occupy their units; and third, to hire and train a staff to run a 300-plus room hotel.

Getting a firm date for the opening proved challenging. It depended on whom one spoke to. Otten insisted that the hotel would open for Christmas 1999. While I was not privy to internal ASCRP financial plans, it was clear in retrospect that ASC planned on cash from sales and operations of the hotel to meet upcoming debt obligations.

It was quickly apparent that the real-estate group had issues internally. Mike Meyers, who was the construction VP, had a notorious temper. Company lore spoke to an event in the Jordan Grand parking lot where Meyers got into a fistfight with the contractor. According to my colleagues who were present during the process of selecting a contractor for the Steamboat project, Meyers, following his overview of the project to a roomful of interested contractors, said, in effect: "I'm going to be the most miserable owner's agent you've ever worked with. I'm going to nickel-and-dime you on everything relative to this project, but the winner who gets the contract will be building a lot of Grand Summits for us."

I was told that following his presentation, everyone left the room except for the PCL team. Only one bidder. They got the contract, and the nickel-and-diming quickly went the other way. PCL had a reputation for being difficult and litigious on change orders, and that turned out to be very much the case. Because of the huge upfront costs involved in each of the Grand Summits (marketing, permitting, then actual construction), perhaps the most critical metric relative to success was accurate final construction costs. That was the baseline for all pricing decisions. Unfortunately, ASC was stuck with a moving target in terms of final constructed costs. Units weren't appropriately priced, and the bottom line eroded or disappeared.

While the hotel was beginning to take shape during the summer of 1999, there was what I would call the "first great ASC financial crisis." In order to meet financial obligations on the real-estate side of the business, ASC determined to identify, and then sell "nonstrategic" properties. According to ASC spokesperson Skip King in April 1999: "We are not being specific on what land we are planning to sell. We have identified $20 million in sellable assets corporate wide."

This effort was led by Mike Krongel, a college classmate of Les Otten's, and a former management trainee at Killington. Mike had actually been Killington's snowmaking manager in the early 1970s but had moved on to other Eastern resorts, eventually landing at Sugarloaf in mountain management. At some point in the early 1980s, Mike decided to exit the ski business and begin a long career in real estate. He joined ASC in 1995, reporting directly to Les Otten as vice president of business development. He was a deal guy and a good one. Looking back, he pulled off a few miracles and allowed ASC to live another day.

What did this mean for Steamboat? Fortunately for ASC, previous Steamboat owners, while not active real-estate developers, had taken the time to subdivide virtually all of the company's developable properties. And these were extensive. Steamboat Ski & Resort Corp (SSRC) at one time owned virtually all of what is now Central Park Plaza, the community's largest shopping center. In 1999, they still owned some lots, including one adjacent to Alpine Bank. Another lot along Right-O-Way ski run was sold to the Christie Club for $1.4 million. An approximately 1-acre parking lot across from the La Montaña restaurant on Village Drive (now the Highmark condominiums) was sold, as well as a parking lot in Ski Time Square, current home of the T Bar restaurant (the owner has not advanced development plans). These parcels were sold during the spring/summer/fall of 1999. In a very complex transaction, Krongel also sold about 40 percent of Ski Corp.'s Gondola Square commercial condominium. In this way, SportsStalker/Christy Sports took ownership of the property they had been leasing. In addition, they acquired what is now "Powder Tools." Gondola General sold to George Noyer, the lessee at the time. The Gondola Pub & Grill were sold to Jim Ellis ... and so on.

While these sales (and those at other ASC resorts) bought ASC some time, the bills eventually came due. Were it not for a large cash infusion of $150 million by Oak Hill Capital Partners in late 1999, the company likely would have entered bankruptcy. One can argue the impact of these sales on Steamboat's evolution as a resort. I tend to be of the view that owners come and go, typically having little effect on the overall appeal or brand strength of a resort. George Gillett and Rob Katz are as different as two executives could be. Both controlled Vail for many years. Minus some griping about the Epic Pass hordes, Vail is still Vail. Otten and ASC have vanished from Steamboat, and the negative impacts have faded over time. In fact, I would argue that the experience of dealing with ASC made the management and staff at Steamboat particularly good at dealing with change, thereby maximizing some opportunities that came their way over time. But with the loss of so many critical real-estate parcels, Steamboat really did weaken its bargaining power in terms of the redevelopment of the base area. In particular, the sale of the Gondola Square commercial space was unfortunate. Ski Corp. lost the ongoing rental income from the sold units, which reduced future cash flows to the company. Also, with so many different owners, the process for redeveloping Gondola Square became exponentially more complicated. The buildings date to the 1970s, and cry out for replacement or updating.

While Steamboat's nonstrategic assets were being sold, the hotel was nearing completion. According to the ASC 2000 Annual Report: "We officially opened our Grand Summit Hotel in Steamboat in October of this year." In reality, a few floors had opened for Christmas 1999 with limited amenities, and it was 10 months later that it was "official," that is, almost completed.

It was also ugly. For all intents, guests and owners occupied a construction zone for that first year. Sales never got the anticipated bounce from the opening. Let's just say that the operating losses were significant. The management team was in place for the full hotel, but only a third of the rooms were available. The strain on the initial management team was such that none continued beyond a few years. The project was not finally complete until December 2000, one year later.

Despite all the angst over the Steamboat Grand, once finished it was a fine property and an important addition to the resort's lodging inventory. Ski Corp. owned the public space, including revenue centers (except street-side retail). For years, the company had used the facilities at the Sheraton for its training, entertaining, etc. Now the Grand could meet those needs.

Even with the sale of "nonstrategic properties" in 1999, the company still struggled under a crippling debt load. This was a double-edged sword, as news of the financial difficulties was well-publicized and certainly impacted the sale of hotel quarter-shares throughout the system. In the case of Steamboat, where publicity was especially negative, fewer than 50 percent of the units had been sold even three years after the opening.

As noted earlier, in August 1999 Oak Hill Capital Partners invested $150 million, giving them a majority of the shares of ASC and opening the door to their eventual ownership. During 2000, ASC had brought in a new Chief Operating Officer, B.J. Fair, replacing Warren Cook, who had left of his own accord, no doubt recognizing the considerable challenges ASC faced. I never thought Warren was very comfortable within the ASC culture, so maybe he'd just had enough.

In a kind of last-ditch effort to preserve Otten's ASC, in December 2000, a proposed merger was announced with MeriStar Hotels & Resorts, which operated several warm-weather properties. According to *The Wall Street Journal* of May 30, 2001, "It seemed the company had solved its long-running cash-flow problems only a few months ago when a merger was announced... But American Skiing gave up its $147 million all-stock bid for MeriStar in late March, citing worsening economic conditions and an inability to obtain favorable financing."ASC took a $3.6 million charge in fiscal 2001 related to the terminated merger.

FIVE DAYS AFTER THE MERISTAR ANNOUNCEMENT, on March 28, Otten resigned. He was replaced as CEO by B.J. Fair. Otten remained on the board, but not as Chairman. He had planned to become chairman of the newly merged company (Doral International). I learned about the resignation from B.J. the night before the announcement. This was not entirely unexpected, given the abruptness of the merger termination. I was quoted in the local paper: "My take is he (Otten) had a lot of hopes on the merger. The word I got is that he definitely had plans to be doing something else. He was going to be getting out of operations, out of the day-to-day operations (of the company). I'm speculating, but when it didn't happen, it might have been difficult to adjust to the change of plans." Sixteen years later, I'd say those comments are still accurate. The public spin from the ASC communications people was that he had decided to move on to new challenges. The truth was a bit more brutal. He had taken his company down . . . and a lot of people with it. I had managed to save an ASC telephone directory from those days. Looking down that list and wondering what happened to all those people . . . well it puts Otten's failure in context.

On March 31, *Steamboat Today* ran a page 2 story: "Otten to be Forgotten." Tom Ross, the paper's senior reporter and one who had been particularly critical of Otten and ASC, wrote about a party being held at El Rancho Nuevo in downtown Steamboat Springs that Saturday night to "celebrate" the resignation:

> "It's a celebration in hopes of a brighter future for Steamboat and the ski area, and a more local-friendly town," said El Rancho Nuevo brew master, David Brereton. Brereton said the animosity toward Otten here was evident in the bumper stickers that sprouted proclaiming "More Steamboat, Les Otten," and on occasion when Otten was booed and heckled in a lift line."

Looking back to 2001, the community's reaction to ASC was understandable. There was real fear that this new ownership group simply didn't understand the Steamboat brand and would cause irreparable damage . . . damage that would then impact their livelihood and well-being. At a visceral level, Les Otten threatened many locals with the idea of who they were. Some identified with the Steamboat brand to the extent that it was who they were. "I live in Steamboat. That's who I am." I'm sure those who showed up had a good time at the "Otten to be Forgotten" party. By then, most people were ready to move on. Others wanted to pile on. Human nature, I guess.

CHAPTER 8

Not So Fast:

Planned Sale to the Muellers

Otten was gone. With the MeriStar merger dead, ASC still faced formidable issues. On May 30, 2001, the company announced its "Comprehensive Plan to Improve Capital Structure and Enhance Future Operating Performance." That came as no surprise. ASC needed a plan. ASC stock traded for $1.17 a share on the day of the announcement, down 9 cents. What was not expected, but happily received by locals and Steamboat employees: that plan included the sale of Ski Corp.

As noted in the company's press release on that date: "This plan represents a fundamental change in the way we manage our businesses," said American Skiing Company CEO B.J. Fair. "It entails a number of significant corporate events, including a strategic asset sale (Steamboat), cost reduction initiatives at every level of the organization, and restructuring of the senior debt of our real-estate company to reduce interest cost and extend amortization and maturity dates."

Ironically, some 10 days earlier, Tom Ross had written an article titled "Intrawest interests only rumor." He had interviewed Dan Jarvis, Intrawest CFO, regarding acquisition strategies and quoted him saying: "Steamboat is definitely one of those on our radar screen." Ross tempered any enthusiasm about

Intrawest's potential interest by mentioning CEO Joe Houssian's comments during an earlier earnings conference call: "We will continue to thoughtfully consider acquisitions, but they're going to have to be great deals to get our attention." Another five years later and Intrawest would be taken private by Fortress Investment Group. In March 2007, Steamboat would be purchased by Fortress and rolled into the Intrawest group of resorts. What a curious, small industry this is!

I mention the Ross article not just because of its eerie foreshadowing, but as reminder of how rumors were flying around regarding a potential sale of Steamboat. Given the Otten years and the financial uncertainty surrounding ASC, this was understandable.

ASC retained Credit Suisse First Boston (CSFB) to assist with marketing the resort. Negotiations between ASC and its lenders bought time for the sales process. Here in Steamboat, we set up a presentation room (dubbed the "war room") in the Steamboat Grand. "The Book" was prepared by CSFB with input from Ski Corp. and ASC executives. As we entered summer, the presentations began, usually one full day in the war room, and a second for detailed tours to familiarize potential buyers with the property. Somewhat to our surprise, there was only one serious buyer, Tim and Diane Mueller, owners of Okemo Mountain in Vermont. Other buyers were generally private-equity groups with little background in or knowledge of skiing.

The Muellers were the most logical buyer for a number of reasons. Most importantly, they were knowledgeable and successful ski-area operators. They knew the business. They also knew the community, as Tim spent each fall big-game hunting in the area. Tim had become involved with the Catamount development in 1996, once plans for the ski-area portion of the plan were dropped. His partners in that project were Lyman Orton, a longtime Steamboat resident whose primary business was the Vermont Country Store back in Vermont, and Nick Schoewe. Nick had a financial background and was running a closely held investment fund with partners from Chicago. Another motivation for the Muellers: their daughter was competing for the Steamboat Springs Winter Sports Club.

The timeline for the sale was to conduct presentations early summer, leave a few months for final negotiations, have a firm contract in place by fall, and close prior to ski season. This is the timeline most ski-resort transactions follow.

Okemo Mountain was family oriented and provided a high level of guest service relative to its competition at the time. Diane personally took charge of all employee training. Her personality was warm and engaging. She was also extremely approachable, whereas Tim could sometimes be aloof. But as a team, they really set the bar for service in the Northeast. They were known for listening, responding, and working well with staff and guests alike. And neither would hesitate to jump in with frontline employees when needed. They had also worked through Vermont's cumbersome development review process (Act 250) with great success, this largely due to their excellent rapport with the Ludlow community, where Okemo is located. Both were deeply engaged with a host of nonprofits. Diane was particularly well respected as an educator and was vice chair of the Vermont State Board of Education. As the Steamboat community began to learn more about them, there was considerable excitement and anticipation relative to the sale. In the popular view, nothing could be more different from ASC than the Muellers.

Everything seemed to be on track until 9/11. The market disruptions that followed put the deal in jeopardy, as the lenders required more equity to go into the deal. The Muellers reached out to a number of Steamboat locals with deep enough pockets to invest. I believe that Orton and Schoewe had been involved as investors from the beginning, but the group got larger. The new entity that would own Steamboat and include the new investors was called Triple Peaks, LLC.

Instead of signing a definitive purchase and sale agreeement in the fall, both parties agreed to a nonbinding Letter of Intent in October. This was disclosed in an ASC filing with the Securities and Exchange Commission, which included the following language:

> The sale of the Steamboat resort is a critical element of the company's strategic plan. As a result, the company is currently negotiating critical terms for the proposed deal and with its auditors are evaluating the effect on its financial statements and related disclosures for the fiscal year ended July 29, 2001, and its credit agreements. In addition, the company is continuing negotiations with other potential purchasers of the Steamboat resort.

It wasn't until February 1, 2002, that a definitive agreement was signed. The purchase price, according to an ASC release on that date, was approximately

$91.4 million for the resort and associated real estate. Not included was the Steamboat Grand. As I recollect, we at Ski Corp. were scratching our heads a bit, trying to figure out how the hotel's quarter-share sales effort could continue, and how the hotel would be managed remotely. But the biggest problem was the timing. As the SEC filing made note, ASC was continuing negotiations with other potential buyers. This reality seemed generally lost to the buyers and the Steamboat community. Once the Letter of Intent had been signed, the Muellers spent most of their time in Steamboat, meeting with employee groups and city and county officials and the U.S. Forest Service (Steamboat operates under a special use permit from the USFS, which was, in effect, the landlord). They had very specific plans relative to capital expansions ($10 million over several years) and were vetting those plans with the authorities.

I was in a very difficult position, trying to facilitate the sale for ASC, my employer, but knowing that sometimes things didn't work out as expected . . . and it might fall to me to keep the train running, regardless of how people felt about ASC. It was clear that I would be moving on, and Tim's son, Ethan, would be playing a major role. So, obviously, I was looking at other opportunities while trying the make sure the deal closed. Looking back, one thing was abundantly clear. The longer it took to close, the more money ASC would need from a sale and the less likely it was that the Mueller deal would work. Each month, the bills were piling up for ASC, but the sale price wasn't changing. I could see a train wreck coming as the Muellers' involvement in day-to-day operations increased after February 1, yet there was no expectation or even awareness that a deal might not happen.

I remember two particularly awkward moments. The first was at the Grand for a winter fundraiser . . . I can't recollect for which nonprofit. At any rate, I ran into Rick Dowden, a Steamboat local and former Volvo USA executive, who was a part of the buying group. Rick is the kind of man who has very high expectations relative to service, and somehow the hotel's valet program had disappointed him. He was quite upset and commented: "Things will be different around here after . . ." OK.

But the strangest moment came when a late arrival to the buying group, Bill Killebrew, wandered into a company management meeting and began lecturing the group on how things would be run post-sale. I had known Bill for many years as someone who was was brilliant but capable at times of rather unusual behavior. This took the cake. The employees in the Headwall Meeting

Room didn't know quite what to make of it. Bill's family had owned Heavenly resort in South Lake Tahoe, but sold it in the 1980s to the Kamori family. He had reappeared in the ski business a few years later as an owner at Eldora, the day ski area outside Boulder, Colorado. Bill's partners were Chuck Lewis, founder of Copper Mountain, and Graham Anderson, an insurance executive with long standing ties to the ski industry. How Bill and the Muellers would work together remained a mystery.

February passed, and then most of March. On March 26, the bomb dropped. I knew that ASC was pursuing backup plans, but, frankly, I assumed that the Triple Peaks deal would eventually close.

According to the company's press release of that date:

> American Skiing Company . . . announced today that it had entered into a definitive agreement to sell its Heavenly ski resort in South Lake Tahoe, California, to Vail Resorts, Inc. The transaction, when closed, will complete the debt reduction component of the Company's previously announced restructuring program. The Company further reported that its Board of Directors had decided not to proceed with the sale of its Steamboat ski resort in Steamboat Springs, Colorado, and will retain that premier resort.

The sale price exceeded the Triple Peaks deal by some $10 million. The announcement clarified that ASC "does not plan to seek another buyer for Steamboat."

B.J. Fair called me with the news before it became public. We both recognized that the staff and greater community would be in a state of shock, and needed to hear the facts "from the horse's mouth," so to speak. B.J. flew to Steamboat the afternoon of the announcement and addressed the staff. His message was that the company's banking partners preferred the Heavenly deal to Steamboat and that drove the decision. Because the banks held liens on ASC's assets, their approval was necessary before any sale could be consummated.

The staff meeting took place in the ballroom at the Grand and was very well-attended. The mood was somber, to say the least. B.J. was blunt in acknowledging the recent turmoil, uncertainty, and disappointment created by ASC within the staff and community. He pledged to work on improving those relationships and to focus on providing Steamboat with the appropriate financial resources to move forward. My sense was that most were hugely disappointed to now have ASC around from a cultural perspective but also concerned relative to having the dollars necessary to continue reinvesting in the resort. Fair made no promises, but made it clear that he felt this sale to Heavenly would lead to more stability in the future.

According to a Q&A with Fair published in *Steamboat Today*: "We have been straightforward and consistent from the beginning regarding our objectives of the transaction—any sale would have to significantly reduce debt. We recognize that both parties worked very hard to make a deal happen that would meet both of our objectives. The timing and circumstances involved are unfortunate, but in the end, the transaction didn't meet our financial objectives."

On the day of closing, Mueller, two of his investors, and his attorney, George Nostrand, were sitting in a Manhattan conference room at the prestigious law firm of Paul, Weiss, Rifkind, Wharton & Garrison, when ASC's attorneys left the room. They never returned. The phone rang in the conference room, and they were told that the deal was off.

One of the local investors was Joe Fogliano, who was quoted in an article on the nixed deal in *Steamboat Today*: "All of us are disappointed," said Fogliano, who learned of the events through an e-mail message Tuesday at about 3 p.m. "We felt like we had a good team. We were backing the Muellers."

Everyone had an opinion. Henri Stetter, a Steamboat local who consults with the World Bank, wrote in a letter to the editor in *Today*: "They (ASC) literally buy themselves a few additional minutes of breathing space. But Steamboat is not out of the hole. ASC still has a major financial problem and in a few months they will have to look again at selling Steamboat. History will repeat itself once again."

Tom Ross wrote an article that appeared on April 1, concluding that, despite the setback and uncertainties ahead, "Steamboat will always be Steamboat." It was hard to believe it then, but time has certainly proven that to be true. Just a week later, Ross wrote another piece reminiscing on "what if Intrawest had purchased Steamboat and Heavenly from Kamori instead of ASC." According to Ross, Intrawest was outbid by $200,000. Former Ski Corp. President Gary Mielke is quoted: "Kamori felt that Steamboat would be in better hands with a ski operator and being American (not Canadian like Intrawest) that ASC would be better accepted by the community and not carry the foreign stigma that had haunted the Japanese ownership years."

Looking back at the Triple Peaks deal, one thing was difficult to accept for those of us in Steamboat: how the Muellers were treated at the offices of Paul, Weiss. Tim Mueller was quoted in Vermont's *Rutland Herald* on March 28: "Nobody with any ethics, nobody, on the day of closing do you call it off," Mueller said. "We don't think this is the normal way to do business, and (it's) why corporate America gets a bad reputation."

I had no idea how the last-minute negotiations were going, but it didn't take a rocket scientist to conclude that to get the best price for Steamboat, there had to be another deal on the table. I get it. And the Muellers knew all along that ASC was pursuing alternatives. I remember speaking very directly to Tim about this. "You know that they are looking at other options," I said. His response: "They wouldn't dare not sell to us. This community would go crazy." So, honestly, I don't think he ever gave it a thought.

What was unnecessary and has colored my view of the ASC leadership at the time was why Tim Mueller got a phone call instead of a face-to-face explanation that another option had been selected at the last minute by the board, with appropriate apologies for bringing them to New York. Not an outcome he would have been happy with, but the message could have been communicated in a more sensitive, civil manner. The Muellers and their investor group were given the high moral ground. As time passed, as will be noted, ASC matured in its management style and began providing capital resources to Steamboat, but memories lingered as to how the Muellers had been treated. I remember Andy Wirth, our marketing VP, saying to me: "I just don't get it. Why did they (ASC) have to do it that way?" I felt the same way.

Tim and Diane bought a full-page ad in *Steamboat Today* on March 29 with just the kind of professional, thoughtful communication one would have expected:

> Although we are truly frustrated and saddened by the recent cancellation of the closing on Steamboat Ski & Resort Corporation, we want to thank you for your support of our efforts to acquire Steamboat. The people we met in the past few months made us feel welcome in a town that we view as an exceptional place to live, work and visit.

We had looked forward to getting to know more of you and to help foster a new relationship between the ski area's owners, the employees and the town.

The community and the mountain have tremendous potential that can be realized through collborative efforts and some much needed capital. We wish you the best of luck as you look toward the future of Steamboat Springs.

Steamboat will always have a special place in our hearts. Our ownership of Catamount Ranch and Club will ensure that we will stay connected to the area, and hopefully our paths will cross in the future.

And so the next generation of bumper stickers began to show up, including "Just Say No to ASC." Triple Peaks, LLC, filed a lawsuit in U.S. District Court in Denver within days of the aborted transaction in an effort to force American Skiing Company to honor the sale contract. Tom Ross, in an article on April 6, quotes Tim Mueller: "We're still interested in acquiring the ski area. That's the main point of the suit, rather than just looking for damages."

The suit was eventually settled for $5.14 million in July of 2004, representing 5.6 percent of the purchase price and substantially more than the $500,000 that ASC asserted was provided for in the contract. Regardless, ASC had the preferred solution and still owned Steamboat.

As B.J. Fair stated in his letter to shareholders in 2002:

Ultimately, it became apparent that selling Steamboat would not achieve our objectives.

During the sales process, we received unsolicited interest in our Heavenly resort that did achieve the objectives we established in May 2001. As a result, we successfully delivered on our goal of reducing debt through the sale of Heavenly in May 2002. We realized an excellent value for the resort and recorded a modest gain on the sale despite a very difficult economic and capital markets environment. More importantly, the sale allowed us to reduce and restructure our resort credit facility to provide the liquidity needed to support our 2003 business plan.

B.J. Fair returned to Steamboat in late May to address the annual Economic Summit. As reported in the May 31, 2002, issue of *Steamboat Today:* Fair addressed Steamboat's business leaders ... and promised increased investment and a less heavy-handed involvement in the resort's day-to-day operations. "We are definitely committed to Steamboat, and we are committed to the Steamboat culture."

With Otten gone, Fair made a number of swift staffing changes at the corporate level. Mark Miller, the COO who had previously been CFO, resigned after his position was eliminated. Two real-estate executives, Hernan Martinez and Peter Tomai, moved on (though not without filing arbitration demands relative to their separation).

Many members of the old Sunday River management team also departed, including Skip King, who had led communications, and marketer Chris Brink. In 2002, the company's executive offices were relocated from Newry, Maine, to Park City, Utah, a physical expression of the fact that the Otten era had ended. Shortly after the company moved into the new office suite, Blaise Carrig notified B.J. that he was leaving to join Vail Resorts as president of Heavenly.

CHAPTER 9

Woodstone Consulting:
Putting the Diamond in the Right Setting

J ust as I was getting strange looks and comments from locals, so were other
employees and managers. The angst created by ASC and the failed sale was
just as intense within Ski Corp. as it was in the larger community. Given the
Otten years and the failed sale, it would be reasonable to expect that the company was experiencing dysfunction. Despite these challenges, a few years later,
in 2007, Steamboat Ski & Resort Corporation would sell for $265 million.
The Ski Corp. that sold in 2007 was a very different company from the one
ASC acquired in 1997.

Ski Corp. had enjoyed a lengthy period of independence pre-ASC. That
world had been turned upside down by the time I arrived in February 1999.
At that time, the pervasive attitude on the part of management and staff was
that they were victims of the new ownership. As victims, they were paralyzed
in their response. My challenge, then, was to call out ASC for its clear management blunders, but at the same time to find a way for the Steamboat managers to take some control over their destiny and begin to manage the
relationship with ASC. While ASC was often wrong, it wasn't always wrong.
And ASC owned Steamboat. Period.

In what was certainly fortuitous timing, I was introduced to a local by the name of Ed Meagher, who owned a small ranch on the Elk River Road called Woodstone Ranch. Ed had been a senior human resources executive with PepsiCo and recently retired to Steamboat and established a management consulting company. The purpose of our meeting was to talk about the Yampa Valley's Community Agricultural Alliance and look at options for serving locally grown beef at the ski area. Ed had volunteered to help the group with its marketing. The conversation quickly steered toward the management issues I was struggling with. Ed described his background working with companies that had faced similar issues. I needed help and Ed was available . . . and so we began a complex seven-year relationship.

There were two distinct silos within the company. Marketing and Mountain Operations folks occupied the fourth floor of the company's gondola building. Human Resources and Finance were generally spread across the third floor. The two groups seemed to align according to their office floors and often fought. I wouldn't say that it was a hostile environment, but you could sense the tension when discussing larger issues as a group. Coming up with a consistent strategy to manage the ASC relationship was going to be impossible unless we could get Ski Corp. management aligned.

In the fall of 1999, we headed out to Ed's ranch and had our first daylong senior management retreat. Ed and I had met several times to plan how to conduct the meeting. We were in agreement on what were the most important messages to convey, and the outcomes we expected for this first session. The priorities were: first, to change behaviors so communication between departments could improve; second, to begin teaching a leadership model that said, "you are responsible for your own success *and* the success of others"; and third, to begin the process of moving the team members away from their victim mindset.

We had all taken the Myers-Briggs test, and then shared the personality profiles with each other at the meeting. Looking back, I think this was helpful in getting the team into a more introspective mode. Each of us has a preference for sharing or accepting information based on personality, so understanding each other's profile is indeed helpful.

Of course, the ASC elephant was on the table the entire day. But when one of the executives would start complaining, Ed was consistent in his response: "OK. I understand the ASC issue. But what could you have done to drive a different result?" We came away with a list of "ASC issues," but also with a second list, which was "what we could have done differently." And so the process of group maturation began. The meeting was not a home run but a good, solid single. As a team, we were beginning to improve our communication internally and were moving out of a "victim" mentality by focusing on what we could control versus what we couldn't.

One lesson that I learned from Ed, and which reinforced my own evolving philosophy on leadership, was that of "musher" management. "You lead from behind," Ed said in describing my personal style. His example was a dogsled team. You provide the direction, make sure everyone is fed, show concern over their well-being, and build loyalty. You make sure you've picked the right dogs for the team, and then get out of their way and hang on. You lead from behind.

I also learned this in the Army, not exactly what you might imagine in terms of traditional officer training. Don't you lead from the front? Well, not in Vietnam. And not in many management situations. The troops were demoralized, often drugged, resentful, and generally ambivalent to authority. "Go ahead, send me home, whatever, I don't give a shit." I'm sure there were a few "strack" (disciplined) units left in 1971, but not mine. Drugs were so ever-present that periodically the MPs would fly in with a team of doctors and nurses to drug test the whole unit.

Shortly after I took over as platoon leader and officer-in-charge for a joint Army of the Republic of Viet Nam (ARVN) and U.S. communications site at Hill 184, the testing team showed up. The result: some 50 percent tested positive for heroin. Seriously?

They were hauled off to detox in Cam Ranh Bay and returned to me one week later, not quite the modern 30-day rehab. This was not a happy bunch. One more failed test and it could be prison time and a dishonorable discharge.

Some cared about that. Others didn't. The heroin, by the way, was so pure that it was smoked as a powder in a marijuana mixture or repacked into a Marlboro. In the latter case, it was impossible to detect by smell. No need to inject. It was so potent and the addiction so strong that I had one trooper who refused to leave when it was finally his day to go home. We found him hiding under his bunk while a jeep waited for the pickup. "I can't go cold turkey. I'm married to the white witch." My first but not last experience with the devil of addiction.

I don't want to overdramatize the challenge. Most of the platoon members were good troopers, followed orders, and maintained a reasonable discipline.

And a number of those who had tested positive were not addicts and just needed a wake-up call. But all in all, this was a pretty dysfunctional group. I knew instinctively that I had to make some immediate changes in their world.

First, I had to convince each and every one that I cared about their welfare and that my job was to get *all* of them home in one piece, and that meant drug-free. Next, I had to distract them for a time so we could focus on relationship building.

The NCOs had to buy into the idea of being closer personally to their charges ... not something that comes naturally. We set up a basketball court behind the latrines where there was enough concrete to have a reasonable quarter-court. Sports are a big deal in the service. I'd learned this intimately back at Fort Sill in Oklahoma, where I had been the athletic and recreation officer for the 214th Artillery Group. One of the best jobs I ever had. And even though this was Vietnam, there was going to be a basketball championship for the Brigade. I wanted some of our guys on the team, and so that became the goal. It worked. Several of them were outstanding, and did make it. We all followed their progress in the games, and several went all the way to Saigon for the finals. It was a healthy, positive distraction.

I changed my schedule so that I spent much of the night wandering around the Hill, checking guard positions on the perimeter and just being visible. I slept when I could. The strategy was to just be there, to demonstrate how much I cared. When a team had to clear brush or cut down tress, I did what many officers would not. I joined in to help. Physical labor. We were in a special situation. We needed a different plan.

If you wanted to know where the Americans were in-country, you just looked to the sky in the morning. They would be burning their "sh...," and black clouds rose from the bases. This work was often done by the native Vietnamese, the *papasans*. In our case, the luxury of having "paid" help disappeared due to security issues.

I had one particularly incompetent staff sergeant on the Hill who could not get with the new program. He wasn't a druggie, but I'm hard-pressed to think of another positive attribute. His incompetence was legendary. So to him went the job of burning the morning refuse. I was down at company headquarters one day when I happened to look off into the distance, toward Hill 184, and there it was, not a black cloud, but raging flames.

I raced back to find the fire barely under control. My problematic staff sergeant had managed set the entire latrine structure on fire by lazily not pulling the honey pots far enough away. That was the last straw. He'd almost burned the whole camp down.

We got him sent away ... I can't remember where. The whole platoon breathed a sign of relief that he was gone. And had a good laugh over the circumstances. We turned the Hill over to an ARVN platoon in April as part of the Vietnam withdrawal, and I went with the remains of our group to the Special Forces Compound in Nha Trang. I remember celebrating with a barbecue, for which I did the cooking. We rode up Route 1 in a small convoy, anxious to be moving on. Morale was OK. We were all going to be OK.

SO I HAD LEARNED QUITE A BIT about "leading from behind," and I was all ears for Ed's training. Some elements were quite basic, but amazingly, very much needed and appreciated. Many years before, I had heard this summary from an executive: "In my 40 years of management, I've never met an employee who woke up, stretched, and said, 'I can't wait to go into work today and screw up.' It just doesn't happen that way!" So true.

We typically fail as managers in providing the right resources, or, and this is equally as likely, we place the individual in a position where success is impossible: wrong skill set, wrong environment, whatever. Ed called this "putting the diamond in the right setting." Instead of focusing on an individual's weaknesses, the discussion should be positive: What are the skill sets required, and is this individual a good fit? If it's the wrong fit, then that's management's problem, not the individual's.

The message was, "Everyone can shine like a diamond when in the right setting." Basic, yes, but something the Ski Corp. team needed to hear at the time, as there were numerous failings in just this regard within the organization.

AT THE OTHER END OF THE TRAINING SPECTRUM, we had very high-level 360 reviews at our annual retreat. The process was fairly simple. We all sat at a large table, and each executive team member would give a summary of how the year had gone and finish with some thoughts on what might have been done differently. This is typically called a "plus/delta" review: focusing on the positive achievements but also acknowledging what we might have done better. After each presentation, everyone at the table would comment on what the individual had said, acknowledging, reinforcing, or offering a different perspective.

On the chapel steps at Middlebury, a scholarship kid majoring in English Lit.

Taking a break in Vietnam with John Kuhl, my roommate from Fort Sill, Oklahoma.

Getting ready to leave Hill 184 and celebrating with a barbecue. That's me, the chef, at far left with the bib.

Pres Smith defined the Killington culture. He's shown here in 1961 with his daughter, Leslie, a future U.S. Ski Team member and four-year All-American at Middlebury.

Pres Smith and Joe Sargent on the roof of the original Summit Hut in the 1960s. They are flanked by Maureen Harrington to the left and Sue Smith.

Leo Denis brought an American-focused teaching strategy to the ski school . . .

. . . and transformed GLM into the Accelerated Ski Method in the "Killington Way."

Pres Smith and his Killington team in 1989, from left to right: Smith, Foster T. Chandler, Marty Wilson, Hank Lunde, Dave Wilcox, Leo Denis, Carl Spangler, and Bob Cook.   KAREN LORENTZ PHOTO

Bob Perry's photos and posters for Killington were legendary, and he got me a ringside ticket to the Ali-Quarry fight!   KILLINGTON RESORT PHOTO

MOUNT SNOW NAMES AND FACES

MOUNT SNOW SKI RESORT
MOUNT SNOW, VERMONT 05356
(802) 464-3333

CHRIS DIAMOND
Vice President/
General Manager

BRUCE McCLOY
Vice President/
Marketing Manager

DAVE BUCKLEY
Assistant Vice President/
Maintenance Manager

DAVE DONNELLY
Operating Manager/
Food Services

RICK KELLY
Operating Manager/
Hotel/Real Estate

PAUL MELLO
Retail Manager

ROBERT 'TIGER' MILLER
Manager/Lift Operations

FRED BAKER
Snowmaking Supervisor

MIKE VILLARS
Manager of Skiing

DEBI BRADSHAW
Office and
Accounting Manager

GEOFF BRYANT
Ski School Director

JAY MORELLI
Golf School Director

Facebook, circa 1978: My first chance to lead came at Mount Snow, where we put a strong team together.

MOUNT SNOW PHOTO

We were successful in refocusing on the skiing experience at Mount Snow. In retrospect, maybe we shouldn't have gotten rid of the Air Car (with Fountain Mountain in the background) and the outdoor pool. But the old bubble lifts had to go. Fountain Mountain hosted race camps into late May.

MOUNT SNOW PHOTOS

Settling in at Mount Snow, where I survived the vagaries of New England weather from 1977 to 1994. MOUNT SNOW PHOTO

Sharing the stage at a black-tie event with Jim McGovern, the legendary innkeeper of the Hermitage Inn. My body language is encouraging him to wrap up his speech.

My "other life:" Racing off Newport, Rhode Island, on Coyote. That's me in sunglasses and hood at the companionway.

Where are we? Consulting the charts on Lake George.

Piloting my Lyman 25-footer on Lake George.

Joining the NSAA board in 1980 opened my mind to national ski-industry issues. This photo was taken somewhere in the Austrian Alps with NSAA executive director Cal Conniff, a superb social chairman.

The Diamond family at one of the annual NSAA national conventions in the late 1980s, with Eileen, Keenen, and Elizabeth.

We were fortunate to persuade Michael Berry to lead the re-constituted NSAA in 1993; his leadership has been invaluable.

At an NSAA gathering with veterans of the industry, clockwise from top left: Hans Geier, myself, Bill Killebrew, Andy Daly, Dick Kuhn, and Irv Naylor.

With its real town and mountain, Steamboat had long been among my favorite Western resorts. I was not the local favorite when I first arrived. Opening the Steamboat Grand was one of the many challenges we faced.

Les Otten was smart and charismatic, but he could not complete the juggling act. Bumper stickers like the one above started appearing in Steamboat not long after his arrival.

KILLINGTON RESORT PHOTO

With hard work, a little luck, and lots of presentations to potential buyers, we took Steamboat from a $91 million valuation in 2001 to a sale price of $265 million in 2007.

Couldn't have done it without you, Eileen.

Bill Jensen was the ideal choice to lead Intrawest in 2007. Then the world changed.

Toasting Steamboat's 50th anniversary with Billy Kidd, the longtime director of skiing.

State of Colorado

Proclamation

WHEREAS, Chris Diamond, a cast away from Vermont, landed in and became a beloved member of Northwest Colorado, and a longstanding community member of Steamboat Springs; and

WHEREAS, Chris shepherded the Steamboat Ski and Resort Corporation through tremendous growth and transition in a business- and environmentally-friendly way for 16 years; and

WHEREAS, Chris served his community on many boards, especially dedicating his time and passion to the Yampa Valley Community Foundation as a committed Board Trustee for over 16 years; and

WHEREAS, Chris has that Vermont intonation and New England lilt; and

WHEREAS, Chris was honored with the NSAA's Lifetime Achievement Award, the industry's highest accolade, for his contributions to the ski and snowboard industry; and

WHEREAS, Chris has made numerous improvements to the Steamboat Springs community because of his great leadership and service, as well as his commitment to the State of Colorado; and

WHEREAS, Oh, and by the way, Chris is an ardent skier and a balanced biker;

Therefore, I, John W. Hickenlooper, Governor of the entire State of Colorado, do hereby proclaim, forever after, June 30, 2015, as

CHRIS DIAMOND DAY

in the State of Colorado.

GIVEN under my hand and the Executive Seal of the State of Colorado, this thirtieth day of June, 2015

John W. Hickenlooper
Governor

I do still have that New England lilt: Governor John Hickenlooper's proclamation making June 30 Chris Diamond Day. It came as a total surprise at my retirement party, and was presented by Sue Birch, a longtime Steamboat resident who is the executive director of the state Department of Health Care Policy and Financing.

Importantly, I would be the last to speak to avoid directing the discussion in a particular way. This allowed maximum honesty. For those who have not gone through a similar exercise, it can be quite emotional. It is also a great team-building exercise, as each individual's performance is validated by the group. Demonstrating fallibility is an important part of the process. For many, there's a lesson in the importance of humility when it comes to successful leadership. Our team needed this.

The next step was to roll out this training to the director-level managers, which happened over several years with at least two different groups. It was important to demonstrate our interest in developing their skill sets and to make sure we were all reading from the same leadership book. At the time, we called this the "Woodstone Model." While the nonsale to Triple Peaks in March 2002 was traumatic, it would have been dramatically worse if the team had not been focusing on how to manage change.

ED MADE ANNUAL PRESENTATIONS to our staff at fall orientations and at the "all managers training." He had exceptional stage presence and was able to deliver a stern message on not being victims ("Let's get over ASC") without alienating the staff. His presentations were always well-received. Changing a culture is a process, and for Ski Corp. it certainly didn't happen overnight. But in two or three years, with Ed's help, change began to occur.

Some on the management team were not comfortable with ASC no matter what, and had moved on. Some executive changes were made as cost pressures continued and we found reorganization opportunities. Some changes occurred because we didn't have the "diamond in the right setting." Bottom line: within four years, we had an entirely new senior management team. In most cases, director-level staff members were chosen to move up, a good thing for the organization and validation for the training that Ed was leading. This new team wasn't "siloed" like the original group, and bought into our new mantra: they were accountable for their own success and also the success of the rest of the team. And their focus was on what they could control, not what they couldn't. "We don't get to pick who owns Steamboat..."

From a personal perspective, the toughest challenge I experienced was in the summer of 2003. It had been a particularly difficult winter for ASC resorts, and the company was still highly leveraged. We had an ASC senior team meeting in Park City, and another cost-reduction plan was rolled out. For

Steamboat, that meant taking another $3 million in costs out of the operation. This on the heels of two or three similar ASC cost-reduction "initiatives" we had already worked through. Given what had happened over the prior four years, I just hit a wall. Driving back from Utah, I called Ed and asked if I could stop by the ranch and talk about it. We sat down in his office, and I began whining about how unfair the new cuts were. He spoke clearly and directly: "Stop whining. You're being a victim. You need a plan, so let's just figure this out."

How deflating to be so wrong. But how important that message was at the time. We eventually developed a plan that achieved the savings but had minimum impact on the company moving forward. In other words, we didn't have to do anything that compromised our future success. Unpleasant, yes, but done.

Unfortunately for Ed, while he was perhaps the most effective management consultant I had ever worked with, and arguably the perfect coach for Ski Corp. at the time, he couldn't "walk the talk" in terms of how his own consulting business was managed.

Ed brought in a number of partners during the years we worked with him. None seemed to stay more than a few years. Most came from companies where he had done consulting work in the past. The ostensible reason: family conflict. Ed had made it clear on many occasions that "family came first." That generally meant keeping his daughters on the payroll when the payroll might not have supported them. But you would have never known there were financial issues with Woodstone. The ranch was impeccably maintained and was a near-perfect setting for serious meetings, plus quality social experiences afterward. A huge family room with a bar and two-sided fireplace. Very expensive Western art everywhere. Separate barn with horses. A veritable sanctuary, and a perfect corporate retreat.

Over the years we worked with Woodstone, Ed completed a number of additions and enhancements to his ranch, including a waterfall feature in the backyard (water-rights issues kept it from running predictably). Each year, our experience seemed to improve on a parallel course with the property upgrades. If I'd noted any issue, it was the constant staff turnover ... excepting family. And Ed was agressively promoting his company, in a manner that just didn't seem appropriate to its scale. He had a first-class location, a lovely complex that was also his home, a solid client base, and what appeared to be sufficient income.

I made the mistake of agreeing to sit on his "advisory" board and talked my friend Verne Lundquist, the legendary CBS sportscaster and a Steamboat local, into joining as well. That was a mistake for which I apologized many times to Verne. After one meeting, we were scratching our heads at Ed's bold self-promotion. He was basically trying to take advantage of this "advisory" board to develop client leads. We thought we were going to participate in creating the next iteration of the Woodstone model. I was getting skeptical, and that skepticism was shortly confirmed.

Tom Steitz, a longtime nordic-combined ski coach for the U.S. Ski Team, joined Woodstone after leaving the team. While the circumstances of his departure were never publicly clear, it wasn't a mutually agreeable parting. Tom was well-known and equally well-respected in Steamboat, because the team had been headquartered there and trained at legendary Howelsen Hill. Until the Salt Lake Olympics, there were no comparable training facilities in the West. Nordic Combined is a small, relatively unknown discipline. Athletes have to compete in cross-country as well as jumping. To succeed, one has to be accomplished at both, a difficult challenge. Tom had successfully developed a talented squad that went from virtual oblivion to frequent World Cup and World Championship podiums. When his team entered the 2010 Vancouver Olympics, the U.S. had won just two nordic medals in its history, one in cross-country and one in jumping. The team Tom had trained brought home four medals, three silver and a gold.

Tom had built-in credibility as an athlete and successful coach, so he was well-suited for leadership consulting. And Tom had actually used Ed's services in Steamboat to help what were very "individual" athletes to focus on their team accomplishments as well. Again the theme: "You are responsible for your own success as well as that of your teammates."

But Tom and Ed's partnership turned out to be unpleasant, with the two of them eventually suing each other. The situation was cloudy and uncomfortable enough that we at the Ski Corp. began to step back from Woodstone. Eventually, Ed shuttered the Steamboat location, leaving the ranch to the banks, and moved to Lake Havasu, Arizona. The ranch remained vacant for many years, and deteriorated at a stunning pace. Around 2010, the Ski Corp. looked at purchasing and refurbishing the property; it was on the market for a pittance relative to Ed's invested cost. But it was a sad scene, and we declined.

Woodstone's failure aside, the leadership concepts that were taught benefitted Ski Corp. immensely, especially when the company went on the blocks again in 2006. By then, it was a company accustomed to change and comfortable in dealing with those challenges. Ed Meagher had been a great resource and, even better, a good listener and coach for me during those tumultuous ASC years. I have immense respect for his talents and, frankly, will never fully understand what happened to his company following the Steitz squabble. I learned in August 2016 of Ed's passing, and wish his family the very best. There are many organizations, like the Ski Corp., that are better places because of Ed's good work.

CHAPTER 10

For Sale Again:

How Did That Happen?

B ack to the ski business. Fiscal 2006 represented something of a turnaround for ASC. On a same-resort basis, the company achieved record revenues. While still leveraged, the company was in a much improved liquidity position. Capital spending was finally growing beyond minimum maintenance levels, with over $26 million in improvements targeted for the 2007 ski season.

One of the achievements in fiscal 2006 was the sale of virtually all of the remaining units at the Steamboat Grand. Real-estate debt had been a sea anchor for ASC, and with the Steamboat auction, that debt was reduced to zero.

The auction also cleaned up the Steamboat balance sheet in terms of a potential sale. It didn't hurt that the Ski Corp. had put up record earnings as well in 2006. In July, it was reported that Bear Stearns & Co. and MainStreet Advisors had been engaged to assist in marketing the ski area for sale. As B.J. Fair reported in the 2006 annual report:

> Our Western resorts' stellar performance, in particular that of
> Steamboat, provided the impetus to review all available options
> for the resort. One possible avenue is the potential sale of the
> resort. We do not contemplate such an option lightly. The
> Steamboat resort and surrounding community have been

exceptionally supportive of our efforts to ensure that the full potential of the resort is realized. While a decision to sell Steamboat is not finalized, such a sale would substantially reduce our outstanding debt balances, consistent with the company's strategy of opportunistic debt reduction when market and operational factors favor such a move. We have worked very hard to position the resort for success in the coming years, whether under the ASC banner or possibly a new owner.

I'm not sure the larger Steamboat community would agree with that statement. Instead of "exceptionally supportive," a more accurate description would have been, "skeptical but hopeful."

Some important improvements had occurred: the replacement of the vintage Burgess Creek double with a new Poma triple; replacement of the Sunshine Triple with a detachable quad (albeit a used lift, transferred from The Canyons); and numerous food and beverage upgrades to on-mountain restaurants.

By 2006, the ASC senior leadership team was beginning to gel into a more responsive and effective organization. Generally, it operated as a matrix organization, with frequent communication between leaders of the various operating departments at the resorts. Food and beverage was one area of particular success. Jim Snyder, who had managed F&B as well as the Grand Summit at The Canyons, became the functional lead for this group and had his hand in all major F&B renovations. The new marketing VP was Chip Carey, a longtime industry veteran, first with Sugarloaf in Maine and, most recently, with The Canyons. Chip was pragmatic and easy to work with, so almost immediately the frustrations experienced by resort marketing teams began to diminish. No more "Magnificent 7s." Randy Howie, the senior IT director at Steamboat, took on additional responsibility at ASC as VP for IT Business Solutions. Another Steamboat executive who took on additional responsibility was Andy Wirth, a tenured, well-respected marketing professional. With Chip Carey's promotion to the ASC corporate team, Andy assumed responsibility for marketing The Canyons in addition to Steamboat.

After a long line of ineffective real-estate executives, ASC placed Stan Hansen (formerly of Heavenly and Mount Snow) in that role. Finally, we had someone who understood the ski-resort business. It would soon fall to Stan to manage the sale of ASC's resorts, something he probably didn't expect when taking on this new position.

BACK AT STEAMBOAT, our management team was beginning to enjoy working with the new ASC folks and very much appreciated their new responsiveness. The small team at ASC clearly enjoyed working with one another. They were finally functioning as a team. Steamboat executives had accepted additional responsibilities within ASC and, as a result, more influence inside the company. What a change from the Otten days.

ASC had a vigorous program to develop corporate-sponsorship revenue, for everything from official resort vehicles to telecommunications and financial services. Given the financial challenges that ASC was facing in 2001, it was amazing that the program didn't completely collapse. That was credit, in my opinion, to the efforts of the program director, Dana Bullen, a former Sugarloaf marketing and sales manager who is now, in 2016, the president of Sunday River. Dana was very much a relationship guy and believed in bringing all the partners together once a year for a social outing that doubled as a sales and re-cruiting pitch.

For many years, this was held in Steamboat. Dana would roll out the red carpet for more than 50 visiting executives. Being a Maine boy, he loved lobster, and the highlight of the annual "Sponsor Summit" was a lobster dinner at Rag-nar's in the Rendezvous Saddle Lodge. Attendees traveled there by snowcat-pulled sleigh, and were treated to a memorable steak and lobster feast at the private party. Dana was the chef for this event, and it seemed like everyone wanted to watch the meal being prepared and share in the process. He also arranged for the sponsor partners to get updates from ASC executives on the financial health of the company, industry trends, etc. His energy and focus kept the program together despite continuing financial crises at ASC. Dana's engagement was especially noted and appreciated by everyone at Steamboat. A few of the sponsors from those days are still around, and talk fondly of their experiences.

My sense was that B.J. and his team really wanted to turn ASC into a vi-able, multiresort ski company. But Oak Hill private equity, now in control, was no doubt looking for an exit strategy. As it turned out, the parts (resort companies) were worth a lot more sold separately than anyone would pay for the entire ASC. Had the "new" ASC been able to continue opertating

for a few more years, that might have been a different story. That's not how
it turned out.

In December 2005, Starwood Capital purchased a majority interest in
Mammoth Mountain, California, for 11 times EBITDA, a reported $365
million transaction. Tom Ross interviewed former Vail Resorts President Andy
Daly in July 2006. In discussing the Mammoth sale, Daly replied, "That's
probably one of the reasons American Skiing retained Bear Stearns to test the
market." I'm sure he meant that in the context that a quality resort could generate such a high multiple, and it might be a good time to sell. There was speculation in the Steamboat community that Vail Resorts was interested in
Steamboat, but that was probably fueled by Daly's investment in a new real-
estate development project, Alpine Mountain Ranch, and his frequent visits
to town.

The 2006–07 ski season was arguably a high-water mark for U.S. destination resorts. Nationally, the top five seasons in history in terms of skier visits
had occurred in the prior six years. The Lehman Brothers collapse was still
down the road. Real-estate values were rising. Ski resorts were viewed as attractive investments based on successful operating histories, with real estate as
a bonus upside. So unlike the 2001 management presentation, where there
was really only one buyer with appropriate credentials, the 2006 sales process
was "frothy."

The abandoned deal with Triple Peaks had led to a lawsuit, which was settled in 2004. The terms of the settlement gave the Muellers 30 days from the
announcement of the next sale process to take part in exclusive negotiations
with ASC. This, of course, led to speculation in town about whether they
would reengage. Mueller was quoted in *Steamboat Today*: "If we decide we're
interested, we'll be serious ... The price, I'm sure, is much different," he said.
"Everything is different." The Muellers had since purchased Crested Butte
Mountain Resort, and were in the midst of aggressive expansions plans on the
mountain and in the base area.

We spent most of that summer working with Bear Stearns and MainStreet
Advisors on the management presentations. It was back to the "war room,"
the Sarvis Creek Meeting Room, at the Grand. This time, the presentations
were much more bullish in terms of growth opportunities (as with the entire
ski business), and let's just say the real-estate market was "hot." One Steamboat
Place was about to begin construction in the base area. That prime piece of

base-area land had been sold several years earlier to reduce ASC real-estate debt. Other major projects were getting under way in Steamboat. The partnership group (Jim Bob Moffett of Freeport-McMoRan and others) that owned the Sheraton resort and virtually all of the Ski Time Square commercial property had decided that it was "their time" as well. So when we began doing tours with our prospective ski-area buyers, it wasn't unusual to have a resort buyer group pass a hotel buyer group. While this led to some awkward moments, the level of activity and interest confirmed how hot the real-estate market was.

As noted in a *Denver Post* article from September 29, 2006, titled "Hot Heights": "As the Front Range housing market continues to cool, many Colorado mountain resort towns have remained searing hot, especially for multi-million-dollar homes... The really high end—$10 million and above—is certainly selling well... Evidence that high-end homes sales are boosting the mountain market can be seen across the state."

Another positive in terms of Oak Hill's timing with the Steamboat sale: capital markets were looking favorably at leisure/resort acquisitions. KSL Capital Partners, a Denver based venture-capital firm led by former Vail Associates, Inc. CEO Mike Shannon, had raised $1 billion to invest in the travel and leisure sector, exceeding its fund target of $750 million (*Denver Post*, September 12, 2006). Adding to the optimism, in August, Fortress Investment Group, a global investment and asset management firm with approximately $23 billon under management, announced its plan to purchase 100 percent of Intrawest Corporation for $35 a share. The total value of the transaction, including the existing debt of Intrawest, was approximately $2.8 billion. That sale price represented a 20-percent premium over Intrawest's closing price on February 27, 2006, the last trading day before the company announced its intentions to explore "strategic options." Sound familiar?

It was reasonable to expect that both Fortress and KSL would be interested in Steamboat.

Steve Lipman led the Bear Stearns team, and while not familiar with the ski business, this was not his first rodeo. Paul Wachter of MainStreet Advisors had been involved with a number of ski-resort transactions. They were very good. I remember one rehearsal, just prior to our first management presentation, when Wachter interrupted us: "Hey, I know this is a good company and well-managed, but leave some room for the buyer to believe he can add value." So noted.

Before presentations were scheduled, interested parties had to submit first-round bids and be selected. As I recollect, this happened in early October, and we began the presentations mid-month, sometimes as many as three a week. We weren't finished until the second week in November.

While there were some big players, the biggest was Fortress. Earlier in the summer, I had met the lead Fortress executive for U.S private equity, Bill Doniger. He had attended a real-estate planning meeting at the Grand, where a number of other Fortress executives (on the debt side of the company) were getting an overview of the "Edgemont" project. Joe Brennan, principal owner of Bear Claw condominiums, had an adjacent lot for sale that was one of the most desirable slopeside parcels in the base area. He had a deal to sell it for some $20 million to a development group that was looking to Fortress for funding. Brennan invited me to a meeting with the developers and their planners, ostensibly to look at potential conflicts with the ski area.

It was something of a setup. I was introduced to Doniger, and we stepped out of the meeting room to visit. Doniger outlined his vision for Intrawest, which was under contract to Fortress, explained that they saw long-term value in the operating side of the business and not so much in the real estate, which had been the Intrawest model. He said, in essence, "We've studied the Steamboat numbers and believe we can use the Steamboat example to enhance profits at Intrawest." He was basically telling me they would be the owner when all was said and done. And he was right.

Joe Brennan's land deal did go through for a reported $20 million. Joe had received an untold number of offers for that property over the years, but held out until 2006. Fortress, through its Drawbridge fund (on the debt versus private-equity side), ultimately wound up providing financing for three major Steamboat developments: Edgemont, Ski Time Square, and One Steamboat Place.

On the day in October when we made our presentation to Fortress, there were over 10 Intrawest folks present, including Chairman Joe Houssian. Joe sat in the back of the room next to a mountain map that we referred to frequently, using a red-laser pointer. Joe was busy working his phone. So I had to ask him a couple times to keep his head down so I wouldn't blind him with the pointer.

That was the day the Fortress deal for Intrawest actually closed. I later learned that Joe was transferring funds while he sat there. It was probably the last time he attended a ski-area related meeting ... although he has since returned (with other Intrawest real-estate folks) to resort real-estate development with a new company called Replay. The Intrawest real-estate development arm had been called Playground. What goes around...

While we made management presentations to a wide variety of companies, some in the ski business, others just representing investor groups, none were as detailed or complex as the Intrawest/Fortress meetings. Intrawest was essentially organized into three divisions at the time: first, resort operations, headed by Hugh Smythe, a longtime resort executive who had cut his ski teeth at Blackcomb, then Whistler; second, the real-estate development group (Placemaking); and third, the real-estate sales group (Playground). Each of these groups was on hand at the management presentation. There was also a timeshare group that focused primarily on Intrawest-developed properties (Club Intrawest). And the company also owned Canadian Mountain Holidays, the iconic Canadian "heli-ski" operator. It was a huge enterprise... the largest ski-holding company in North America. In Colorado, it owned Copper Mountain and controlled Winter Park through a long-term lease agreement with the City of Denver.

During the management presentations and meetings that followed, it was clear that Fortress was evaluating not just Steamboat but the Intrawest team as well. Visualize a three-sided meeting-room table: Ski Corp. and ASC folks at the head of the table making the presentation, Fortress on one side, and Intrawest on the other.

The Intrawest acquisition team returned in December just prior to the holidays for a week of intense due diligence. On December 19, Intrawest announced that it had signed a purchase and sale agreement with American Skiing Company to acquire Steamboat Ski & Resort Corp. Included in the deal were the commercial core of the Steamboat Grand and the Walton Pond Apartments (staff housing).

"The acquisition of Steamboat represents another milestone in our long-term strategy to develop, market, operate, and provide our customers with access to the world's premier network of experiential destination resorts," said Alex Wasilov, president and chief operating officer of Intrawest, in a company press release. "This acquisition marks the resurgence in our strategy to grow through acquisitions and to leverage our platform to enhance value for our customers throughout the Intrawest network of resorts." The purchase price of $265 million included approximately $4 million in assumed debt. For ASC, this transaction cleared up all senior debt and outstanding revolver balances in ASC's senior credit facility and other indebtedness (for clarity, excepting amounts owed Oak Hill).

As would be expected, the reaction from the Steamboat community was uniformly positive. A March 9 editorial in *Today* proclaimed: "Steamboat Springs let out a collective sign of relief Thursday when Intrawest officially sealed the deal to buy the Steamboat Ski Area."

And why not? Given what had happened in 2002, when American Skiing Co. terminated its agreement to sell the ski area to the Muellers on closing day, it's hard to blame the community for being a little leery.

"We have said it before: Intrawest is the kind of buyer the community hoped for. It has a proven track record in the ski industry, owning or operating 11 successful ski resorts in North America. Contrast that with ASC, a company that had been just a year old and on the front end of its rapid expansion when it bought Steamboat in 1997."

Oak Hill could not have picked a better time to test the market.

Once the Steamboat deal was signed, other ASC resorts followed. On February 16, Mount Snow and Attitash were sold to Peak Resorts for $73.5 million. Four days later, ASC announced it was selling Killington and Pico to SP Land Company for $83.5 million. The Maine resorts quickly followed, with much speculation about whether Les Otten would reappear as an owner. That didn't happen. By late June, ASC had announced its intent to dissolve and in July filed with the SEC to do just that. Even with these assets sold, ASC still owed Oak Hill some $404 million. According to an article published in the July 3, 2007, *Today*:

> The timing of the dissolution coincides closely with the due date of redemption of the preferred stock shares in the company, all of which are controlled by Oak Hill.
>
> The sale of Steamboat and the Maine resorts didn't raise sufficient funds to pay off Oak Hill and other creditors, thus the company informed the SEC there would be nothing left for common shareholders.
>
> Even after selling off all but one of its ski areas, ASC still owed Oak Hill $404 million . . .

Don't feel sorry for (Oak Hill), McCurtain (Brad McCurtain of Maine Securities Corp.) said. "If they don't come out of it whole, they'll come awfully close."

McCurtain said Oak Hill has been able to make the terms of its loans to ASC and the interest rates it collects on them.

This interest burden effectively eliminated any chance for payback to shareholders.

The Canyons was eventually sold in July 2007 to Park City real-estate developer Talisker Corp. for $100 million. With that, ASC quietly slipped away. Most of the small executive-leadership team had been absorbed into The Canyons operation or had moved on.

At the time of the Steamboat sale, the real-estate market in Steamboat had been heating up along with the rest of Colorado. One Steamboat Place and Wildhorse Meadows were about to begin construction. Projects like Trappeur's Crossing and Cimarron were selling out, and prices were escalating. You can bet that savvy brokers were emailing clients about the sale. Adding to the froth, the Sheraton and Ski Time Square commercial properties were being sold, the Sheraton to Starwood Resorts (already a minority partner) and Ski Time to Cafritz Interests. Everyone could see the likelihood that the base area would finally be brought into the modern-resort era.

CHAPTER 11

Working with Intrawest:

Getting Smaller, Day by Day

So began a very busy transition period for Steamboat. The P&S had virtually no contingencies, so a March closing was anticipated by both parties and deemed extremely likely. Our team at Steamboat had been working closely with the local Urban Renewal Authority (URA) relative to a planned base-area promenade. Prior to the promenade construction, the major culvert carrying Burgess Creek through the base area had to be replaced. Then Ski Corp. had to complete a regrading of the Headwall, removal of all chairlifts, and then installation of a new detachable six-pack and a relocated triple chair (Preview). This was a huge task and required precise engineering, as the new grades would have to match that of the promenade. All utilities and snowmaking would also have to be reconfigured and replaced. In order for the promenade construction to begin as planned, these improvements needed to be substantially complete by fall 2007. ASC had committed to these investments, and now Intrawest would be obligated if the URA improvements were to move forward.

Ski Corp. had done the initial Headwall design work with SnoEngineering out of their Frisco, Colorado, office. Intrawest had a long-standing relationship with Ecosign, a Canadian planner, so once the sale was complete, we were encouraged to switch planning firms. This was an awkward time. Ecosign was well-respected, so getting their view on the Headwall project would be helpful. The challenge was timing. It was March 1, and we needed to start moving dirt almost immediately, order the lift, etc.

After their first visit, it was obvious that Paul Mathews, the Ecosign principal, and Hugh Smythe, Intrawest president of the Mountain Resorts Division, didn't like the plan we had already vetted through ASC and the authorities: a six-person, detachable chairlift with an angle station. The angle-station unload would serve Headwall beginner terrain. Those who chose not to unload could continue to the top of Christie Peak, providing a significant enhancement for out-of-base capacity. There were three short, old fixed-grip lifts on the existing Headwall, and the simplicity of the plan was that capacity could be increased and the lift "clutter" reduced with the proposed configuration. The ancient Christie II double chair would also be removed. The primary concern of Intrawest was that Steamboat didn't have enough out-of-base capacity, and fixing that was a priority. They proposed a new lift running from the base to the vicinity of Vagabond Saddle instead.

Steamboat is unlike many destination resorts in that there is not a large day-skier component. No one comes to Steamboat for just the day ... it's too long a drive from Denver and other major population centers. This means that "staging" (the process of moving through the base area and then accessing the upper mountain) takes place over a roughly 3.5-hour period. Except for powder days, there are few folks waiting in line when the lifts first open. The resort staff felt strongly that Steamboat skiers did not want to access the mountain via Vagabond Saddle. Many of the veteran lift staff already had experience with a similar lift concept ... terminating "Arrowhead" below Thunderhead peak ... and it was such a bad idea that the lift was eventually removed. It was felt that the long-term issue of "staging" could be dealt with when the existing gondola was replaced.

Doug Allen, our VP of mountain operations, was at wit's end. He kept providing more and more information, but couldn't get a decision from Hugh. Finally, I interceded with David Barry, who had been promoted to chief operating officer of the U.S. resorts in February. David seemed to agree with us but also could not get a decision from Hugh. Eventually, I had to appeal to Doniger. With that we had a decision ... to stick with the original plan.

This was my first experience with Intrawest's internal politics. I could see that there were going to be challenges. Barry was frustrated with Hugh Smythe and wanted his job. Fortress wasn't sure what kind of organizational structure they wanted. Alex Wasilov, new to his role as CEO, was trying to work with the new Fortress ownership and integrate Steamboat. It was not clear that he was going to be around long-term. These were interesting times. It was especially difficult for us at Steamboat because we were "last-in" to the Intrawest portfolio, and it had been post-Fortress. Everyone knew change was coming, and there was considerable anxiety. Not in the financial sense, as the senior Intrawest executives had enjoyed a big payday via their stock holdings when the Fortress purchase went through.

Intrawest was very much a Canadian company. Virtually all senior executives were Canadian. Many had moved across the border via acquisitions. David Barry, for example, ran Copper Mountain following its purchase by Intrawest. His original major ski experience was at Tremblant, as I recollect. The Intrawest team had grown up in a unique (to the ski industry) culture. As Intrawest was initially a real-estate development company, the ski areas were viewed as amenities and improvements to those amenities were seen as a value add to the real estate. Two extraordinarily successful projects were Tremblant and Whistler/Blackcomb. In both locales, the company was able to create virtually brand-new base villages without the issue of legacy buildings or uncooperative landowners. These became state of the art and effectively set the bar for base-area development in North America. Ironically, I noted the following in the 1998 ASC Annual Report, where the company is describing its real-estate strategy:

> Each resort village creates a pedestrian environment where guests can be accommodated in attractive new lodges, or shop, dine and be entertained for the length of their stay without need for transportation. Our goal is to create an experience of leisure convenience. Each of these resort villages is currently in the master planning stage and ranges in size from as much as 5 million square feet for development at The Canyons to approximately 1 million square feet of development at Heavenly during the next 10 years...

This could have been taken directly from any Intrawest Resort sales brochure. Intrawest's resort-village development model was being copied all over. If you were the ski-resort operator at an Intrawest Resort, you had incredible resources. Rather than fighting for minimum annual capital spending to keep your facility running, Intrawest lavished new lifts, snowmaking, and infrastructure on their resorts to raise their overall appeal. In a way, this explained Hugh Smythe's desire to consider new out-of-base lift options for Steamboat, regardless of the cost.

It was a model that Intrawest rolled out to other properties following their acquisition. Stratton had a small base village, Copper's was larger, with relocated parking and drop-off areas designed to drive arriving guests through the village on their way to the slopes. This was a key Intrawest development strategy, designed to ensure base-village vibrancy. It was employed at Winter Park, using a Cabriolet (open gondola) to carry guests from remote parking to the base village, but at a distance from the main slopes in order to, again, drive traffic through the base village. Unfortunately, when implemented south of the border, none of these plans worked quite as well as the Whistler and Tremblant models.

Both Copper and Winter Park struggled to find tenants for all the commercial space. It was becoming clear that resorts with multiple parking lots and access points were challenged to match the same retail experience or energy as Tremblant or Whistler. One size didn't fit all. For Winter Park, the new Cabriolet lift took guests from a day lot to the resort base . . . but at an inconvenient location relative to lift access. A family of four didn't care about shopping at 9 a.m., they just wanted to get to the lifts as quickly as possible. This challenge was similar to The Canyons (now a Vail Resorts property), where the Cabriolet required an inconvenient hike to access the main mountain gondola. The gondola base was eventually relocated to shorten that walk. Another obvious point in comparing the Whistler/Tremblant villages to Copper/Winter Park . . . the Colorado resorts simply didn't have enough lodging units to support a major village. Perhaps the commercial village development got ahead of the bed base.

But these were minor issues in the context of Intrawest's reputation as resort operators and developers. As it was primarily a real-estate company, that's where a large chunk of the Fortress valuation went, even though Fortress executives spoke publicly about the long-term value being in the operating side of the business.

So just as Oak Hill's timing with the sale of ASC assets was fortuitous, Fortress's timing was about as improvident as you could have. Lehman Brothers collapsed in 2008, and resort real estate, once a driver of valuation, became essentially a nonproducing asset on the balance sheet of each ski area.

Fortress had put significant equity into the Intrawest deal, and had confidence enough in their strategy that long-term financing was not part of the plan. The deal was done using equity and a short-term bridge loan. When that loan came due, the credit markets, post-Lehman, were in turmoil. And so began a rapid, multiyear "shrinking" and repurposing of Intrawest.

Just before the Great Recession struck, Fortress determined to replace CEO Alex Wasilov with a ski-industry professional, consistent with the strategy to create value by focusing on operations. They were able to attract veteran resort leader Bill Jensen. Bill had most recently worked for Vail Resorts, where he had been copresident of the Mountain Resorts Division, one of the most visible, influential positions in the ski industry.

Bill, in my judgment, was an ideal choice to lead Intrawest forward and extract value from its operating versus real-estate assets. He had started his ski-industry career at Mammoth in the lift department, and spent time at Sunday River as marketing VP under Les Otten. He also gained experience working on the supplier side of the industry as president of Kässbohrer NA, a prominent European manufacturer of slope-grooming vehicles (PistenBully). He moved on to become president of Northstar in Lake Tahoe, where his organizational skills and consumer focus garnered him national attention. During his tenure, Northstar was respected as one of the best-managed resorts in the Sierras.

As I recollect, he took several executive MBA courses during the Northstar stint and took advantage of the opportunity to be mentored by senior Fibreboard (Northstar's owner) executives. I had known Bill for years and wound up working closely with him in the late 1990s while attempting to sell Bear Mountain (owned by S-K-I Ltd.) to Fibreboard. They seemed the logical buyer, and while the negotiations were lengthy and sometimes painful, the deal eventually closed. It probably would not have happened if he hadn't been sitting on the other side of the table.

Bill eventually moved on to the Vail Resorts group, at Breckenridge, and then Vail itself during the Andy Daly leadership period. Rob Katz eventually stepped in as CEO, and Bill, as noted, became copresident of the mountain resort division (sharing leadership with former Intrawest executive, Roger

McCarthy). By this time, Bill had experience with all major U.S. markets and was well-known to suppliers, operators, and the media. I can't think of anyone who had a comparable breadth of experience, and I actively promoted him to Fortress. He was a proven operator and well-connected in terms of his ability to open doors and assist Intrawest's growth through acquisitions.

Within the Intrawest real-estate division there were two silos, the development side and the sales side. The developer group had done numerous villages in North America and was moving forward internationally, with projects as far afield as Hawaii, Mexico, and France. The developers were supported by a large sales team with demonstrated success stories in terms of "launch" sales for individual projects. At the time in 2007, it would be fair to say that Intrawest was known primarily as a resort real-estate developer and secondarily as a ski operator. And they were held in high regard by the larger real-estate community.

For the first year and a half that Intrawest owned Steamboat, I had to make numerous trips to Vancouver or Whistler for planning meetings. At those meetings, Fortress was represented by Toby Ippolito, who reported to Bill Doniger. Looking back, I think Toby was trying to understand what they had just bought (including Steamboat) and how the new organization should be structured . . . and hoping for direction from Doniger.

It was a very chaotic time. While the overall resort real-estate market was still hot, things were changing. Challenges existed within both Intrawest real-estate silos: the development group was having issues with cost overruns or legacy building issues, while the sales group was not hitting targets. Meetings tended to devolve into excuses and apologies on the real-estate side. One challenge for new ownership was simply appreciating the extent of Intrawest's holdings, which ones made sense to hold and which should be sold off. At a high level, the Fortress strategy seemed to be to focus on improved operations at the resorts (with no additional acquisitions near term) and, on the real-estate side, to simplify the business model and understand which projects were profitable and which were not. And then adjust the business plan accordingly. This probably would have taken three to five years. And Jensen certainly had the skill set and motivation to make it happen.

BUT THE WORLD CHANGED. The Lehman collapse in the fall of 2008 brought a hard stop to resort real-estate development. On the ski operations side, as the recession deepened, the impacts were more manageable. Skiing and boarding remained popular, and profitable, despite the economic crisis.

For Bill Jensen, it was a whole different challenge. Instead of fine-tuning operations and increasing profitability at North America's largest ski company, he had to move into survival mode. I remember him saying, "This wasn't exactly what I signed up for."

Shifting back to a Steamboat perspective, the first 18 months of Intrawest ownership had been a flurry of activity. We had new financial resources with which to execute our plans. As noted earlier, we completed the total renovation of the "Headwall" lift and trail system. The base-area promenade was complete, and while we still had the old Gondola Square to deal with, overall the ski base area had never looked better. There were three major base-area development projects moving forward: One Steamboat Place and Edgemont were under construction in 2008, and all of Ski Time Square and the Thunderhead Lodge were in the process of being demolished (excepting only the infamous Tugboat bar) in anticipation of redevelopment . . . possibly to include a Ritz-Carlton. Plans were being vetted for redevelopment of the old Best Western Ptarmigan lodge adjacent to One Steamboat Place.

Off mountain, the Wildhorse Meadows project was moving forward with its Trailhead Lodge. West of town, "Steamboat 700" was working through the permit process. This project was essentially a second town, requiring annexation by the city in order to provide utilities and services. Even downtown Steamboat was in on the development party. Three new, very-urban condo projects were coming out of the ground: Howelsen Place, The Olympian, and the Victoria. Utilities and roads were going in for a new subdivision: Steamboat Barn Village, located north of the hospital grounds. There were a number of other projects being planned, but you get the picture. The vacation-home real-estate market had never been hotter. Post-Lehman, the market softened but did not come to a grinding halt as quickly as in other places. As had often been the case over time, Steamboat joined the real-estate boom later than most resort towns in the Rockies, so not illogically, it was one of the last to see the slowdown. But as the calendar turned to 2009, sales eventually dried up.

Looking back from a 2016 perspective, there were dozens of locals and second-home owners who lost large sums of money through foreclosure, and many who are still "under water." Speculating on real estate wasn't just a corporate strategy. But it is remarkable that the Steamboat community endured this real-estate transformation with relatively little impact to the larger economy and, specifically, the ski-travel business. Not that it wasn't painful for the individual developers, real-estate sales folks, and those in the construction trades. Unless a project had very deep pockets, ownership soon transferred to lenders.

One that transitioned from the role of lender to that of owner was Fortress. Not the private-equity group that owned Intrawest but the debt/distressed-asset side, called Drawbridge. Fortress had provided mezzanine debt for these projects and eventually wound up in the driver's seat . . . like it or not, for One Steamboat Place, Edgemont, and the Ski Time Square redevelopment project. It took until 2016 for One Steamboat Place and Edgemont to essentially sell out. Ski Time Square has yet to see a new unit constructed, although I have noted that Fortress is now actively marketing the Ski Time Square/Thunderhead property. While the economy continues its slow improvement into 2016 and the home-building segment is finding strength, the resort housing market is in only the early stages of recovery. There are those who say resort real estate is on the rebound. Equally, there are pundits who argue that the market will never be what it was. I wouldn't bet on that. People aspire to live in or retire to our wonderful mountain communities, and that demand will eventually translate itself into new projects. One fundamental change is the disappearance of speculation buyers. Today's practical customer intends to regularly use their mountain property as a vacation home, which ultimately creates a healthier, more sustainable community—and market.

For the Intrawest real-estate group, the Great Recession meant the end of a phenemonal run. The situation in Steamboat, which I described above, was essentially repeated at each property in ski country. No resort was spared. The more committed to real estate as part of the business model, the more negative the impacts. Jensen and his real-estate lead, Brian Collins, identified a "scrap heap" of assets that needed to be disposed of as quickly as possible. Unfortunately, they weren't the only ones selling. That said, over several years and under the cloud of a possible bankruptcy, they began the disposition. It included ski resorts as well as real-estate assets. Panorama, B.C., was sold, along with Mountain Creek in New Jersey. Copper Mountain as well. The most painful disposition was that of Whistler/Blackcomb, which was spun off via a public offering in Canada. Whistler had always been the gold standard within Intrawest. It was where the company cut its teeth in the ski industry (evolving from a real-estate development group). Most of its senior ski executives worked through the ranks of that resort . . . the largest in North America. Intrawest maintained a minority position for a few years, but eventually sold its remaining shares.

As an operator of one of the remaining resorts, my instructions were to help the company first to survive, then stabilize its business, and then begin to grow again. Capital funding dried up for all but required major maintenance projects. Everything downshifted from a growth model to intense cost controls, including staff reductions, hiring freezes, etc.

Déjà vu all over again.

With Intrawest on track to become a modest holding company of five resorts, with a 50-percent interest in a sixth (Blue Mountain, Ontario), the CMH heli division, Club Intrawest, a handful of hotels (Hawaii, Mammoth, and Blue Mountain), and other miscellaneous investments, Jensen closed the Vancouver office and relocated the headquarters to Denver. Vancouver office staffers were offered the opportunity to relocate, but virtually none did. The new offices were designed to hold just over 100 staffers, a number which Bill believed should reflect the size of the corporate office going forward . . . to keep its cost from draining off the cash its operating divisions were providing. All real-estate activities had been shuttered and the staff released. Intrawest was a now a Denver-based, New York (Fortress)–owned operating company in the ski business. Much smaller, but still alive.

IN JANUARY 2014, Intrawest went public on the New York Stock Exchange, with Fortress retaining ownership of some 60-plus percent of the shares. Bill Jensen and Travis Mayer, the executive VP for operations and business development, were totally immersed in the process from late 2013 until the actual offering took place in January of 2014. According to reports, they were well-prepared and made excellent presentations.

The result was a $12.00 per share offering price. The mood within the company brightened noticeably as both Bill and Travis settled back into day-to-day management of the business. The company had moved from survival to growth mode. Capital became available and the mindset shifted to "How can we add value?" It had been six difficult years, but all in all, an amazing story of survival.

Following the public offering, the big question seemed to be whether

Intrawest would remain as a holding company, with a lean corporate office and decentralized operational model, or begin to centralize to best control costs and then grow through acquisition. There were several initiatives in the acquisition area, but none that closed. As resort operators, we got mixed messages. Jensen, during the office-relocation days, was clearly on the side of decentralization. But the office staff began to grow, especially on the finance, marketing, and IT side. IT had been subcontracted to a Vancouver firm (that had hired many former Intrawest staffers), but that experience had been largely negative. On the marketing side, Jensen had brought in Ian Arthur, a former Vail marketing executive with longtime Colorado roots, including a stint at Frontier Airlines.

Ian was committed to growing and managing the company's guest database and embarked on a number of IT-based solutions to support that strategy. Few performed as hoped, most notably a "Salesforce" investment. He was dragging along skeptical resort marketers who could see problems everywhere, but Ian had Jensen's confidence. We resort folks were told that our marketing VPs now reported to Ian, with a dotted line to the resort chief. Virtually no one was happy with this now-public arrangement. Ian was gone after about three years.

Other changes were being made to the corporate senior team. In a very short period of time during 2014, after Ian left, the Chief Financial Officer (Dallas Lucas) also left and was replaced by Gary Ferrara. Then Jensen himself departed in November, just prior to the ski season, and within a few months, the Chief Legal Officer was also gone. The new CEO was Tom Marano, a career Wall Street executive with senior-level experience at Bear Stearns, and then Ally Financial's Residential Capital mortgage unit, which he led as CEO from 2008 to May 2013. Res Cap was one of the country's largest sub-prime lenders and entered bankruptcy in 2012. Marano had no prior experience with the ski industry other than home-ownership at Stratton Mountain and Park City and a love of the sport. The announcement included the appointment of Sky Foulkes, president of Stratton, as COO. I can say with some assurance that Sky, knowing that he was stepping into the new role, was probably the only person within the Intrawest resort-management group who saw the Jensen departure coming. In the Denver office, the team seemed to be in a state of shock. Then on January 14, 2015, Gary Ferrara left and Travis Mayer was appointed executive VP, CFO, and treasurer. In my view, appropriately, as he was probably the only person on earth with an Olympic silver medal in mogul skiing and a Harvard MBA . . . and an intimate knowledge of the Intrawest business model.

As I write this in August 2016, the Intrawest stock (SNOW) is trading at around $15 a share on the heels of a $50-plus million dollar "dutch auction" or share buyback. The company has announced a number of major capital investments at its resorts and enjoys a strong enough balance sheet to complete both internal investments and the share buyback. The fallout from the executive-office turmoil is in the rearview mirror.

CHAPTER 12

NSAA's Evolution:

The Early Years

Way back in 1980, when I was still at Mount Snow, I had joined the board of the National Ski Areas Association. This was an honor. I would be representing both our company (Sherburne Corporation) and the Northeast region. It was also an opportunity to network with other professional operators and to help shape strategies for the big challenges of the moment: skier safety, liability, government relations, and especially the complex relationship between ski-area operators on federal public lands and their landlord, the U.S. Forest Service. NSAA also played the lead role in establishing and updating the national standard for ski lift operations (B77).

NSAA was formed in the spring of 1962 at the Area Operators meeting held in conjunction with the National Ski Association convention at The Broadmoor hotel in Colorado Springs. The minutes of that meeting provide fascinating insight into the challenges that the industry was facing at the time. The sport was growing by leaps and bounds, but there was no structure by which the area operators could address common concerns, particularly the issue of managing injury claims and securing affordable insurance. At the time, the National Ski Association provided the loose umbrella under which all industry groups could gather, and it included a hodgepodge of regional ski area groups. NSA had produced the NSA skiers code, the first attempt to define on-slope behaviors. According to the minutes, Bill Lash, president of the Professional Ski Instructors of America (PSIA), noted that "the out-of-control skier is quite a problem" and it needed to be controlled. In additional to skier safety, risk-management issues were a priority topic. Fifty-four years later, and not much has changed, at least in terms of challenges.

One of the attendees was David Rowan, who worked out of his offices in New York City. In the minutes, David speaks to the need for a publication to serve the ski-area operators and takes on this task as a service to the new NSAA. The meeting ends with a consensus to move forward with the publication, which would be called *Ski Area Management* (*SAM*); recruit new members via existing regional organizations; establish a New York office; and hire an executive secretary. That individual turned out to be David Rowan. Shortly thereafter, his wife Ann, assumed the role.

David Rowan played a central role in the successful formation of NSAA. At the same time, he forged a business relationship that provided for his family's ownership of what became a successful, industry-focused publication. So his were not altogether altruistic motives. They were in his legitimate self-interest while providing a critically important tool for growth of NSAA and the sport. Per the minutes, *SAM* would provide a page that would function as NSAA's newsletter. The financial success of *SAM* would depend on the growth of NSAA member areas, their buying power, and by extension, the advertising revenue from businesses that sold products to ski-area operators. So the interests of *SAM* and NSAA were supportive, but not necessarily aligned in all respects. This became an issue during the SIA/NSAA merger years and, later, when NSAA began publishing its own magazine.

NSAA quickly coalesced around the goals and objectives set at the Broadmoor meeting. David Rowan, and then Ann, helped in those early years. Following Ann, there was a bit of a misstep, and the individual hired to lead the association was terminated by then-Chairman Jay Price. Price then turned to Cal Conniff, a regional media personality and general manager of Mount Tom in Holyoke, Massachusetts. Cal was recruited as president and executive director and promptly established new offices in his hometown of Springfield, Massachusetts. Cal had practical industry experience, as well as seasoned marketing and communications skills. These allowed him to successfully guide NSAA's growth in those early years.

By the time I joined the board in 1980, NSAA was well-established, running successful regional and national trade shows, conducting educational seminars, and generally being the public voice for ski-area operators in America.

I WOULD DESCRIBE THE BOARD in those days as exceedingly collegial. Most were directly involved in day-to-day operations. Some were owners or majority owners. Others were, like me, the first generation of managers representing a more complex ownership structure. There were few companies with multiple resorts (my company—with Killington, Mount Snow, and Sunday River— was one of the few). In accordance with the bylaws, representation was regionally diverse.

There were, however, two clear camps: the older, longtime directors who tended to be founders or early developers, and those who were relatively new to the business and trying to develop a career. The older board members were accustomed to a stunning level of micromanagement that led to long and often chaotic board meetings. In the early days, the association's budget was small and there were limited staff resources. Most work was done by committee. But by the mid-1980s, Cal had assembled a capable team, and it was time for the older board members to let go. The situation was aggravated by the NSAA's succession rules at the time. They basically allowed the politically favored to move slowly through the leadership ranks and thereby enjoy a tenure beyond what was reasonable. It often seemed to me that the longer someone had been around, the more boorish their behavior.

I remember Tom Corcoran, founder of Waterville Valley and a past chairman, making Cal switch rooms with him at the National Convention when he discovered that his was smaller. Ugh. Cal had a warm, Irish, accommodating personality and sometimes he was just downright bullied by some of the senior board members.

Despite their length, meetings were both an opportunity to keep abreast of the big issues and a chance to relax away from the intensity of day-to-day ski operations. In those days, pretty much every resort chief worked a seven-day week during the winter. A day off tended to be an afternoon, assuming no crisis de jour. So NSAA provided an opportunity to vent steam and escape the day-to-day grind.

Cal Conniff was a superb social chairman. Some board chairs made it clear that this was to be about having a good time, and keeping a lighthearted attitude toward the business. That board contingent was led by Jay Price, president and part-owner of Boreal Pass on the Donner Summit. He was absolutely intolerant of seriousness, and while chairman he gave Cal clear direction relative to social activities: the more the better. What always amazed me about our gatherings was how genuinely everyone seemed to enjoy each other's company.

In the 1980s, the ski-industry leadership wasn't exactly a poster child for diversity. All board members at the time were white males. A "Spouses Committee" met at least annually to make sure that there were plenty of things for the "spouses" to do while meetings went on at the annual convention. My wife, Eileen, and Valerie Cleary did this for what seemed like a very long time. During the Nashville Convention, the major "Spouse" activity was a fashion show downtown. The ladies were joined on the bus, as they always were, by Jay Price, the only male. Jay always preferred to spend the day with the women rather than attend meetings. That particular day he was a surprise participant in the actual fashion show. He found a dress that fit but had to borrow high heel shoes from Abby Killebrew to complete the outfit. Jay would drive Cal nuts. NSAA eventually joined the real world, and the "Spouses Committee" is history.

During my board tenure, Conniff organized two trips to Europe. They were great fun, but also incredibly educational: visiting legendary resorts, plus tours of lift manufacturers, grooming-equipment manufacturers, etc. My first trip to Europe included a visit to Zermatt, Switzerland, to ride the new Klein Matterhorn Tram. Prior to arriving in Zermatt, we had visited several lift manufacturers, including Von Roll, which built the new lift. We had also been to the CWA plant, where the two Tramway cabins had been built.

We were told that the Klein Matterhorn lift had the longest section of unsupported lift cable in Europe, about 1-mile long. It was absolute state of the art, and something we all looked forward to seeing. It had taken several years to build, and reportedly, three men had died during construction.

The lift literally terminated inside the rocky summit. Engineers had carved out of the rock enough space for the top terminal and unload platform. The downhill side was a sheer rock face, and so the last few minutes of the ride felt as though one was in an elevator, going almost straight up. To get skiers to the slopes, a tunnel several hundred feet long was constructed, literally through the mountain.

We had to ride at least one tramway to get to the base of the new lift. There, we met a delegation of local authorities, who were on hand to greet the visiting dignitaries and describe the construction challenges. All told, we were about 60 strong. We loaded into the tramway cabin, which, as I recollect, could handle over 120 skiers, and off we went. I wound up standing next to a Von Roll engineer we'd met at the factory a few days earlier. He had been one of the contructon supervisors. We began chatting, and I remember commenting that it must have been quite the sense of satisfaction when the lift was finished and he took his first ride.

"Yes, Chris, but it was also a very sad day," he responded. He then went on to explain that the first ride was similar to today's, in that the cabin was packed with local officials, lift company executives, etc. Included was the mayor's mother. He lowered his voice and pointed to where the mayor was standing in our car … just a few feet away.

"When the cabin arrived at the unload, all the excited passengers disembarked and headed toward the tunnel. Except for the mayor's mother, who was one of the last to unload. Instead of heading left and following the crowd, she went right and fell from the unloading platform, hundreds of feet down the rock precipice and into the glacier."

It wasn't until the following summer that they were able to retrieve the body. The Klein Matterhorn was a marvel of lift engineering and construction, but on its first day of operation, no one had thought to erect a barrier to prevent just such an accident.

I share this as one incredible story, but also because it captures something about the European spirit and disdain for the kinds of safety precautions we are accustomed to in America. That said, I did note that the area from which she fell had been sealed off with a veritable wall of steel mesh.

TRAVELLING WITH FELLOW SKI OPERATORS was always an adventure. The kind of people who commit their lives to the ski business are invariably interesting characters: risk takers, outdoor enthusiasts, and people who are passionate about their work. As noted, Cal was an exceptional social chairman, and he arranged nuymerous outings for the board. We even travelled several times to Bermuda, following an official board meeting in Washington, D.C., or another mainland-based locale. There were a lot of pranksters on those early boards, and meetings were always entertaining. If there was a catalyst in terms of the fun factor, it was our attorney, David Cleary.

On a visit to Washington in the mid-1980s (probably about a public-lands issue), I remember attending a reception in the Dirksen Senate Office Building with Cleary, Jerry Groswold, the public lands chair at the time, and Cal Conniff. We were leaving the reception at about the time office workers were heading home, so as our elevator descended, staffers would pile in on each floor. After one stop, Cleary shuffled over to Conniff, pulled out a wad of $100 bills, and announced in a heavy Southern accent to everyone: "Well, Senator Claghorn (Conniff in his suit and appropriately round paunch did look the part), we sure do appreciate all your help on the floor today." And with that, he began peeling off hundreds and stuffing them in Cal's pockets. Well, at the next stop, the packed elevator basically emptied as all the congressional staffers ran for cover. We roared with laughter in the empty elevator.

CHAPTER 13

NSAA 2.0:

From Stepchild to Industry Leader

But times change. In 1990, NSAA merged with SIA (Ski Industries America), the trade organization representing the product-manufacturing and retail side of the ski business. The new combined entity, a merger of equals, was the United Ski Industries Association (USIA). The total revenues of businesses represented by the new organization were approximately $4.5 billion, with each of the former two groups accounting for about 50 percent. With that merger, Cal Conniff retired, and the Springfield offices were closed. The president of SIA, David Ingemie, became president of USIA.

Just two years later, this marriage ended in divorce. What in the world happened? Hindsight is always 20/20. There were, in my view, four dynamics at work in the NSAA decision to merge with SIA.

First, the Western resorts of NSAA were growing their businesses at a much faster clip than the rest of the membership. Many in leadership out West longed for a more visible and effective presence in Washington, particularly on public-lands issues. Our lobbying effort at the time was led by the American Ski Federation (ASF) and its president, Joe Prendergast. ASF was theoretically an umbrella organization for all elements of the industry (NSAA, SIA, National Ski Patrol, and Professional Ski Instructors of America). NSAA and SIA provided the bulk of the financial support. ASF was pretty much a one-man lobbying show. On the ski-area side, the heavy users of Joe's services were the Western areas with water rights, Forest Service, or NEPA issues. There were no other significant initiatives, such as a national public-relations effort. Many on the NSAA side felt that the SIA offices in McLean, Virginia, would provide for a stronger Washington presence. And, it was felt, the merged entity would have more clout, both political and financial.

Second, while SIA and NSAA had combined in the past on a number of marketing efforts designed to drive awareness and participation in the sport, none of these brought measureable success (one exception was the "Bring a Friend" campaign, more on that later). Those on both sides who were looking for new, more vigorous demand-building initiatives believed that a merger would lead to more effective marketing and growth in the sport. The joint marketing strategy began to take on a life of its own ("Ski It to Believe It"), and this marketing program evolved on a parallel track to the merger. "Ski It to Believe It" didn't drive the merger, but it greased the tracks.

Third, there was a feeling on the NSAA side that the staff at the current NSAA Springfield office was not up to the task of leading the industry into the 1990s and beyond. This opinion was most strongly shared by the large, Western resort members and by those engaged with the NSAA Marketing Committee working on "Ski It . . ." and other programs. With the notable exception of Irv Naylor of Ski Liberty and Roundtop in Pennsylvania, most of the Eastern resorts were ambivalent about the merger. Irv had issues with the Springfield office and was highly supportive.

In the case of my company (then S-K-I), executives were highly supportive of the Springfield office and skeptical of the merger. Of my Killington cohorts, Pres Smith and Hank Lunde felt strongly that this change would result in significantly less influence for the East. Foster Chandler, on the other hand, was deeply involved with the new marketing efforts and more supportive. In summary, it would be fair to say that all in, the NSAA side was accepting but not enthusiastic.

Fourth, each side saw the ski world and its place in it differently. NSAA leadership looked at the cash cow that was the SIA annual buying show and, frankly, lusted to put that money to work more effectively to grow the sport. On the SIA side, I think the membership viewed the area operators as a generally unsophisticated lot who would benefit from their leadership in the marketing arena. Looking back, these different views of the benefits of the merger simply highlighted the huge cultural divide that eventually led to divorce. SIA had a long history of ineffective marketing programs, but was open to new strategies. NSAA had never attempted a substantial national demand-building effort.

The metrics and logic of a merger were presented by McKinsey & Company, a global management consulting firm. For weeks, the two negotiating teams met at the Chicago O'Hare Hilton ... always in the Amelia Earhart Room that, in those days, could be quickly accessed from the airport terminal. The senior executive representing NSAA was Jerry Groswold, the president of Winter Park in Colorado and current chairman of NSAA. Jerry became the first chairman of USIA and was to be followed by John Stahler of Tecnica and Volkl (leadership alternated). John's company was headquartered in West Lebanon, New Hampshire, and imported high-end race boots and skis; John was a Dartmouth grad and former ski racer. His view of the trade association was that the board provided broad direction to staff, but beyond that, they were focused on their individual businesses and intent on not micromanaging. He supported the merger, as I recollect, but I don't believe he was prepared for the amount of time he would wind up putting into his role as chairman, particularly in dealing with some outspoken and highly opinionated ski-area folks.

Each association attorney (Shaun Corette for SIA, David Cleary for NSAA) sat in on the negotiating sessions. Cleary had done a great job leading the NSAA skier-responsibility initiative over the prior decade-plus. Thanks to his efforts on behalf of NSAA members, a large majority of ski states had legislation providing some reasonable protection to operators by establishing that there were inherent risks to the sport. He helped draft the NSAA Skier's Responsibility Code, which continues to define the code of conduct on the slopes to this day.

Cleary was skeptical. Given that the offices would be moving and that most of the legal activities were trade (import issues) or SIA trade-show related, Cleary would be stepping away from day-to-day involvement and Corette would be in-house counsel. Fortunately, Cleary memorialized his skepticism in the breakup provisions of the merger agreement.

ONE OF THE MORE VOCAL CRITICS OF THE MERGER, before and after, was David Rowan. David was publisher of *SAM*, the dominant trade publication at the time. Rowan had been very involved with the initial formation of the association, and his wife followed him as its second executive director. His magazine was excellent, bringing useful information such as lift-maintenance best practices as well as resort news. The large suppliers to the industry (lift manufacturers, groomers, snowmaking equipment, etc.) were his major advertisers and key to the financial success of the publication. His concerns around the merger centered on potential lack of influence by suppliers given the larger entity, and possible negative repercussions to the success of both the magazine and trade shows. His concerns were legitimate.

Almost immediately, there were issues with not only the annual trade show but with regional shows as well. NSAA produced two winter regional shows (East and West). While resort chiefs and maybe their marketing leads might attend the national show each spring, the winter regional shows were an opportunity for midlevel managers to kick the tires. They could check out or test-ride the new snowmaking and grooming equipment and attend meetings on timely subjects to improve their effectiveness as resort managers. The shows just weren't as successful as in the past. It wasn't through lack of attention from the USIA staff. They were just flat. There was a disconnect, real or perceived, between the new organization and the NSAA members. Attendance began slipping, and the 1992 spring convention saw a record low attendance. NSAA members were voting with their feet.

Somehow, the emotional connection that ski-area operators enjoyed with NSAA had been severed. While Springfield was hardly an ideal location for the association's offices, it was something of a gathering place, at least for Eastern operators. The staff was accessible, friendly, and always helpful. SIA's offices in McLean became the USIA HQ. Only Dennis Harmon, a senior finance executive who had worked at several ski-resort companies, joined USIA from the NSAA operators' side. All of the former NSAA staff transitioned to new adventures.

In retrospect, we grossly underestimated how the loss of these longtime staff relationships would challenge the new organization. As noted, it was painfully obvious in terms of how the USIA trade-show staff managed the NSAA shows. Suppliers were especially unhappy, as they had lost their former contacts at NSAA . . . and the most important piece, driving attendance, was also a failure. Looking back, while David Ingemie had been a competent lead for the SIA group for many years and had an appreciation of the resort operators' challenges and needs, he was never able to make a strong emotional connection with the NSAA members and bridge the gap from NSAA to USIA.

ON THE MARKETING SIDE, the USIA marketing committee, led by Bill Stenger, president of Jay Peak in Vermont, brought "Ski It..." from an idea to a marketing program ready to be funded and executed. And so the troubles began. To move the needle, millions of dollars would be required for a national program. While the SIA membership quickly agreed to a funding mechanism on their side, there was no such progress with the ski-area operators. Everyone seemed excited with the concept but unwilling to go with a mandatory funding strategy, fearing this would pull the organization apart. So we tried to move forward on a voluntary basis. Even the larger resorts, which had played key roles in developing the program, balked when it became obvious how the new commitment would sap existing marketing dollars. NSAA members had no option, other than reducing their own marketing budgets, while SIA had the trade show. In retrospect, the ski-resort group simply didn't have the financial resources to pull off a major national program. While much has changed from 1992 to the present, it is still hard to believe that today's ski-area operators, enjoying a very healthy business environment, could successfully fund the kind of national advertising program contemplated in 1992. We were and are too small an industry.

FORTUNATELY, FOR ALL INVOLVED, when it became obvious that USIA was a failure, there were a lot of adults at the table and the separation was handled in a very cordial and professional manner. We were all motivated to get our respective segments back on track for success.

David Cleary, the NSAA's special counsel, had done an excellent job protecting NSAA in the organizational agreements relative to USIA. The separation protocols were clearly documented and in order to ensure that NSAA could effectively reconstitute itself. NSAA had continued to function as a shell throughout the USIA years, conducting brief annual meetings, electing officers, etc. David never said, "I told you so." He didn't need to.

Jerry Groswold had been NSAA chair when the merger started and I was vice chair, so I moved into the chair role following Jerry. It fell to me to reconstitute NSAA once SIA gave notice of its intent to separate.

Money was the first challenge. SIA's vote to separate was driven by more than general unhappiness with the merger. There was legitimate concern by their leadership that NSAA's needs were causing a financial drain on the organization (exacerbated by poor attendance at trade shows). And the amount of time that both Stahler and Ingemie were spending on NSAA issues was probably considered excessive and a distraction. At the time of the merger, NSAA had only a modest cash reserve and that cash was rolled into USIA. The merger docs provided for a return of that cash, subject to adjustments, but as I recollect, it was not a large number. SIA agreed to provide a bridge loan to cover expenses related to rebuilding NSAA. Stahler was gracious and accommodating on virtually all separation issues. Had there been any lack of good faith in assisting us to rebuild, NSAA would be a very different from what it is today.

Sid Roslund moved over to the new NSAA payroll as its only employee and, operating out of the McLean office, held things together throughout the rebuilding process. Three things needed to happen. First, we needed to take a fresh look at the NSAA bylaws. As mentioned earlier, there were two membership groups that felt disenfranchised in the old NSAA: small areas (particularly in the Midwest) and industry suppliers. We needed to take a hard look at how these groups were represented. Second, we needed to hire an executive director. And third, we needed to find an office.

To put some structure to the challenge, we formed an informal leadership/communication group based on board membership and logical regional representation. I still had my day job running Mount Snow. Fortunately, I had great support from Pres Smith and the S-K-I Ltd. team and my Mount Snow cohorts. For the year following the separation, I probably spent half of my time on NSAA issues while my colleagues covered for me at Mount Snow.

The very ad hoc leadership group was:

>   Chris Diamond (Mount Snow, Vermont) Northeast
>
>   Danny Seme (Snowshoe, West Virginia) Southeast
>
>   Jerry Groswold (Winter Park, Colorado) Rockies
>
>   Ted Motschman (Mt. La Crosse, Wisconsin) Midwest
>
>   Gary McCoy (Mammoth Mountain, California) West Coast

Each of us was responsible for communicating with members in our regions. We had no formal structure to fall back on, so the telephone was the tool *de jour*. Copies of the old bylaws went to each, and we actively sought input from the membership on changes.

Feedback was consistent across the regions. What we heard was loud and clear: "Broaden board representation, change the process of succession, and break up the good old boys club." Members wanted an opportunity to engage at the NSAA leadership level. The emerging view of a new NSAA was that it should more open and inclusive. While meeting with the membership and talking about the future, a consensus also emerged relative to governance protocol that helped with our selection of an executive director. Almost without exception, members recognized that the old modus operandi of strong committees and overly engaged board members needed to morph into a more professionally led organization with board members providing strategic policy direction and communicating with their regional constituents. Not drilling down into the details of association operations.

Getting feedback from the suppliers required a more politically complicated track. Meeting with David Rowan shortly after the separation announcement, I reviewed our plan for rebuilding NSAA. As David had played such a large role over the years, I hoped for his support. I didn't get it. He stated flatly that there was no way that we would be able to reconstitute NSAA. Obviously, he was looking for an alternative structure that would provide the supplier group and *SAM* a new and more significant role. It was one thing to provide suppliers a larger voice in our organization, but quite another to share leadership.

Fortunately, Rick Spear, the president of liftmaker Poma of America, quietly assumed the role of "supplier negotiator" and worked with us on rationale proposals for change. Rick understood that NSAA was fundamentally an association of ski-area operators and that was not going to change. The new bylaws eventually provided for an additional supplier board seat. Additionally, we created a trade-show committee with broad supplier representation. That committee, which functions to this day, ensures that NSAA is provided an appropriate forum for supplier members to present their products to NSAA members.

Our second challenge, hiring an executive director, turned out to be fortuitously painless. The whole ski world knew we were looking for a leader, but it would be fair to say that there was some reasonable angst by candidates over the long-term viability of NSAA. While that might have been the view from the outside, NSAA Board members and those involved with the rebuilding were highly confident in our future. We utilized the same headhunter, Buffy Filippell, who had done work for the merger (Ingemie went through a formal interview process, competing with others who aspired to the position) and for U.S. Ski Team executive searches.

The interview team included me, Gary McCoy, and Nick Badami. There may have been others, but my memory fails me here. Gary was president of Mammoth Mountain and vice chair of NSAA. He would follow me in the leadership role. Nick was CEO/principal of Alpine Meadows, California, and Park City, Utah. Nick had spent many years on the NSAA Board and was a past Chairman. Badami was the "B" in BVD underwear, so Nick brought sophistication, experience, and significant political clout to our little industry. Despite his wealth and complex business interests, he was incredibly approachable. Sharp as a tack, but with a wonderful sense of humor, Nick led the interview team. His blessing would be important to whoever finally got the nod.

And that was a surprise. While we generated a huge pile of applications, very few were qualified. We settled on interviewing three. One had planning experience in the industry but no operational background. Another was a successful, retired professional athlete looking for something different, but with no evident, transferrable skills. The third was Michael Berry, president of Kirkwood ski resort in California.

WHILE I DIDN'T KNOW MUCH about Michael, Nick and Gary had worked closely with him on issues related to California politics and the U.S. Forest Service and were impressed. Also, Larry Jensen, who was doing business development for S-K-I Ltd. in Killington, spoke highly of Michael. That said, I was very concerned that we really had only one viable candidate as we went into the interviews. This is not a situation one likes to be in, especially given the daunting tasks ahead. I asked several times if our group felt comfortable going ahead or if we should go back out, shake the tree, and look for other qualified individuals. Nick basically told me to calm down. "I think you'll like what you hear."

He was right.

Berry graduated in 1969 from Franconia College in New Hampshire.

Growing up north of New York City and skiing Hunter Mountain, he caught the ski bug at an early age. I suspect that had some role in his college choice. Following Franconia, he went to work at Hunter Mountain in the snowmaking department. During the winter of 1974, Hunter hosted the NSAA Eastern winter show. A huge contingent arrived from the West, wanting to learn more about snowmaking. Hunter had one of the industry's largest snowmaking plants, and Berry gave the facility tour during the show. No doubt as a result of that tour, he was recruited by Vail in the spring to become their first professional snowmaker. He then went on to Sun Valley, gaining experience in lift operations, and then to Keystone. He eventually wound up at Kirkwood in operations and took over as president following the departure of Fred Jones in 1983.

KIRKWOOD IS ONE OF THE MOST BEAUTIFUL alpine ski venues in America. The terrain is challenging, the views stunning, and the snowfall ... well, just take whatever South Lake Tahoe gets and figure that Kirkwood gets almost 50 percent more. In big snow years, residents exit their homes from the second floor ... and climb up! This is a wonderfully romantic experience (if you're young) but year after year, it can be oppressive. Yes, there is such a thing as too much snow. Roads are closed. Staff can't make it to work, etc. Michael had married by this time and had an escape option to Minturn (about an hour drive away) where his wife's family resided and he had purchased a home. But he was ready for change. Night after night, snowbound in Kirkwood, with occasional visits to the family ... he was ready. Motivation is important.

Michael had exactly the operational experience we looked for, plus a sensitivity to the industry's regional differences. And he was politically astute.

I don't know to this day if he was aware of the lack of competition for the job. We met the candidates at the Renaissance Hotel at the old Stapleton (Denver) Airport. We didn't need much time with the other two candidates. Michael, by comparison, demonstrated an awareness of the political and financial challenges we faced in reconstituting NSAA and clearly looked forward to the challenge, not to mention the escaping Kirkwood part. He was well-known and had the kind of industry relationships that would prove helpful in the rebuilding. He was able to think beyond the immediate challenges of a new office, hiring staff, etc. To this day, I'm not sure if he knew how weak the competition was ... he just needed not to screw up the interview.

We asked him back into the room and quickly hashed out the employment details. This might have been the easiest check our headhunter ever earned.

Not wasting any time, Michael and Jerry Groswold headed over that afternoon to nearby Lakewood to look at an office opportunity that Jerry had discovered. While I was focused on the leadership-selection process, Jerry Groswold had agreed to lead the task of finding new offices. The NSAA Board substantially agreed that Colorado was our logical home. It was our largest ski state in terms of skier visits by a large margin. It was conveniently accessed, and that access would improve with the construction of the new Denver International Airport (DIA). Jerry Groswold was unquestionably the most politically connected of the Colorado ski executives, since Winter Park was owned by the City of Denver ... not to mention Jerry's family and their deep roots in Colorado's ski culture (Groswold Ski Co., etc.). I learned many years later, after taking the helm at Steamboat, that Jerry, as a young attorney, had been one of the original incorporators of Storm Mountain Ski Corporation (later Steamboat Ski & Resort Corp.). He was Secretary and I'm sure provided valuable advice to founder Jim Temple.

Jerry looked at number of options, but the most logical turned out to be a building in Lakewood that housed both the National Ski Patrol and Professional Ski Instructors of America. Office space was available in the same building, so with Michael's agreement, we quickly signed a lease. Jerry was successful in securing a material cash contribution from the City of Lakewood to assist in establishing the new office. He was also instrumental in securing a line of credit from First Bank and was assisted in that effort by Tom Ptach, formerly with Vail, and then, briefly, USIA. At the time, Tom was setting up an office-supply business in Steamboat (where he still resides) but remained very helpful to Michael in those early days. Looking back, Jerry Groswold was certainly the most important resource for Michael. He could open doors anywhere in the city and he did. One of the shared anxieties over a Colorado office was the potential for undue or inappropriate influence from the state's very strong trade association, Colorado Ski Country USA. Jerry sat on that board and made sure that relationships remained professional. While Jerry's contributions to Colorado skiing are well-understood, his role in reestablishing NSAA is probably underappreciated. Jerry was a great friend and mentor. It's with great personal sadness that I note his passing on Thanksgiving Day 2015.

NSP and PSIA, led by Stephen Over, were also great resources to our NSAA team, providing administrative assistance, helping to set up databases, etc. Sid Roslund relocated to Denver. Between the cash from Lakewood, our bridge loan from SIA, and the line of credit, we had enough cash to cover operating costs and office setup until dues began flowing into the new organization.

MICHAEL GAVE NOTICE to his Kirkwood employers and negotiated a transition plan that had him working part-time in the Denver offices beginning December 1 and full-time on January 1, 1993. An immediate challenge was conducting the winter trade shows scheduled for Keystone and Mount Snow, not to mention the national show scheduled for San Diego at the Town and Country. According to Michael, he discussed the position of Manager, Trade Shows and Conventions, with Tom Moreno, who was part of the SIA trade-show team. Moreno declined but recommended that Michael talk to Tom Moore, who at the time was working for the National Automobile Dealers Association in Washington, D.C. Tom and Michael obviously connected, as Tom joined the NSAA team as its first new hire in December. He serves in that position to this day, and there can be little doubt that his competence in reestablishing the tradition of successful trade shows made Michael's job a lot easier.

The Keystone and Mount Snow shows were a huge success. The small NSAA team included Michael, Sid, Tom, and a newly hired controller, Alyson Bradley.

ONE OF THE MAJOR CULTURAL SHIFTS incorporated in the new bylaws was a change in the reporting of the association president. That position reported to the Chair, not to the board. While a somewhat subtle change, the purpose was to make it clear to the entire board that meddling with the leadership would not be tolerated. Michael Berry was the hired professional. It was his task to lead the organization. The board would provide strategic direction and communication would be between chair and president. There were open meetings to discuss the new bylaws at the winter sessions. Gary McCoy, as vice chair, led those important meetings. Feedback was generally positive and the final drafts were distributed to the membership prior to the San Diego annual meeting, where they were adopted.

While the supplier group had received a second board seat, there were still a number of issues from their perspective. The NSAA staff focused on listening to their issues during those early shows. One issue which resonated was the frequent scheduling conflicts between trade-show hours and other sessions. Suppliers wanted to be able to participate in the educational opportunities these shows provided, but, more importantly, they didn't want to sit in their booths in an empty trade hall while buyers were elsewhere. This was an easy accommodation and has served the organization well for some 20 years. As mentioned earlier, a Trade Show Committee, led largely by suppliers, provides ongoing input to staff on any issues, potential show locations, etc.

The following appeared in the Spring 1993 NSAA Member Update, highlighting the issues and challenges the organization faced as it headed into the San Diego Convention.

A Message from the Chairman
By Christopher Diamond, NSAA Board Chairman

On Tuesday, March 2, in Las Vegas, John Stahler and I signed the agreements relative to the separation of NSAA and SIA from USIA. All cash due NSAA, contracts assigned to us, and physical assets have been transferred out of USIA.

As we look to the future and the challenge of rebuilding NSAA into a vital and responsive trade organization, we should not lose sight of the lesson learned from our USIA experience. Since this is my moment in the bully pulpit, here are my thoughts on the those lessons:

- Cultural differences between operators and manufacturers are so deep that joint efforts need to have clearly defined purpose and fit the strategic mission of NSAA. ASF qualifies. Undefined marketing co-ops do not.
- We need to stick closer to our roots—particularly to the needs of the small-area operator, where the bulk of new skiers are first introduced to the sport.
- We need to recognize that our effort to develop a national marketing program was *not a failure*. Many aspects of the program worked and there is much left on which to build. The advertising component *was a failure* because we did not generate the required economic systems to make it work.

- We need to give Michael Berry and his new staff some
  time to put things back together. Let's not forget that in
  terms of many programs and member services, we have
  essentially lost three years.
- We need to quickly reinvigorate our commitment to skier
  education.
- We need to get non-members onboard. The challenges
  facing the ski industry require a strong, unified voice—
  one that speaks for all operators, not just 60 or 70 percent.

Enough of the serious stuff. The convention and trade show
promises to be exciting, educational, and FUN. Let's provide
some energy and focus for NSAA.

While San Diego was well-attended, the hotel was somewhat run-down
and in need of maintenance. Nonetheless, a good time was had by all, celebrating the re-energized NSAA. The bylaws were adopted, allowing a new
board to be seated. As noted earlier, the major changes were expansion of the
board (24 to 28); establishing new regions for proportional board representation; and clarification that directors must be owners, general mangers, or pres-
idents and serve three-year terms, but no more than two consecutive terms.

NSAA staff priorities coming out of the convention included a review of
the committee system that had served the association well for many years but
had virtually collapsed during the USIA era. To accomplish this and continue
momentum for the organization, Michael became quite the road warrior, visiting individual areas and regional organizations across the country. One complaint, especially sensitive to smaller, Midwest operators, was the lack of
presence by NSAA's past leadership on their turf. Looking back, I think his
willingness to travel wherever and whenever built credibility in the new organization and hastened its growth.

While the early years in Lakewood were busy as the team focused on the
basics, the new board set clear direction that we needed to keep an eye on
growing the sport. I think there was a huge risk that the team would just stay
in the moment, rebuilding the association, and lose sight of the big issue:
the potential shrinking of our participation base. To the credit of Michael and
his team, they kept this on the front burner, eventually reaching out to a

Boulder-based research firm, RRC Associates, for help in tackling the issue. There were all sorts of demographic studies sitting on the shelves at NSAA and SIA, but little that was actionable. We didn't know what the demographic trends really meant to *future* participation. And, therefore, we had no idea how to develop appropriate strategies. In the late 1980s and '90s, the ski-resort industry had been given a few gifts that drove increased participation: the shaped ski, snowboarding, and aging Boomers who continued to ski beyond their predicted dropout date. But there were challenges that, if not addressed, would have a significant negative impact on the industry.

Credit goes to Michael Berry and his NSAA boards. The 1990s became the decade that created NSAA's "Model for Growth," arguably its most significant achievement. The 1996 Charleston Convention was a watershed moment in the sense that NSAA members stepped back through a series of visioning sessions and identified the key influencers the industry would face in the next five to ten years. This process ultimately led to the adoption of the "Model for Growth" in 1999. In my judgment, it was NSAA's leadership during these years that set the ski-resort industry on a sustainable path for growth.

Earlier, I had mentioned the role that David Rowan and *Ski Area Management* played in forming NSAA. In recognition of *SAM*'s commitment to provide a communications tool for NSAA, a "noncompete" had been negotiated back in those early days, whereby NSAA was prohibited from publishing its own magazine until 1996. Clearly, in order to bring appropriate messaging to its members, NSAA needed its own vehicle. It began publishing its own newsletter in 1993 and, eventually, a four-color magazine, the *NSAA Journal.* Telling the story of the "Model for Growth" was just one of the many opportunities that the new magazine provided. David Rowan was highly critical of this initiative, but that could have been expected given the potential economic consequences to his family. That said, *SAM* perseveres to this day as a highly successful industry publication, capably managed by David's daughter, Olivia.

LOOKING BACK AT THE USIA ERA from today's perspective, it's truly amazing how the ski world has changed. NSAA focused intensely on its priorities: government affairs, safety and risk management, and investment in a database that would allow prompt responses to the inevitable crises that the industry would face. By way of example, when the tragic skiing deaths of Michael Kennedy and Sonny Bono became international news, NSAA was positioned to respond promptly and accurately to questions regarding skier safety, thereby steering the dialogue in a positive direction. NSAA developed significant credibility as a responsive, professional organization through its handling of these and similar crises.

While NSAA continued to execute on its mission as we entered the next century, the ski-resort business was changing. Resorts were increasingly operating as vertically integrated businesses, managing all aspects of the guest experience. This led to significant improvements in guest service as well as increased profitability. Through various economic cycles, ski-area operators had learned how to do more with less. Ski resorts across the country were steadily increasing profitability and financial health. From today's perspective, many of the risks have been wrung out of the business ... excepting weather.

One area of dramatic change was on the retail/rental side. For skiers and riders taking a destination ski vacation, the quality of equipment available became such that there really was no need to bring your own. That provided additional flexibility in terms of the ability to change skis (or boards) as conditions changed. For an Eastern skier, especially, the ability to grab a pair of wide skis on a powder day was a great option. Other changes included the appearance of high-end service companies, providing in-room delivery and fitting for guests. Here in Steamboat, the first to provide that service was Black Tie Ski Rentals. Now there are a half-dozen other competitors in that space: Ski Butlers, Door 2 Door, Ski Delivery Express, etc. The traditional rental shops have been forced to respond to this new competition by upgrading their equipment, shop functionality, and overall service levels. So the consumer is the winner.

The airlines also handed destination resorts a huge gift when they began charging exorbitant fees for bulky ski gear. The math simply drove one to the resorts' rental shops, where high-quality equipment was readily available. According to NSAA sources, the ski-resort industry saw a shift of about $400 million in retail and rental/demo sales from city-based specialty retail stores to resort shops. Looking at sales from a national SIA perspective, the top line number didn't changed. The math is fairly simple.

And that business is highly profitable. The resort can buy high-end skis and bindings at wholesale for, say, $600. The equipment is rented for $40 to $50 a day. It's not unusual for the ski investment to be paid off by early January, and to see 40 to 60 days of rentals during the season. In the spring, it still has value and can be sold as a "used" demo for half off. The resort shop can generate $2,000 to $3,000 from the $600 investment.

Consider what the manufacturer might have made on that sale to the resort. Of the $600, perhaps $150 represents actual profit margin. I'm not sure what the exact number is, but directionally that's accurate. Clearly, the ski resort operator is generating exponentially more dollars from the transaction than the manufacturer, by a factor of five or ten. I don't think any example better demonstrates the shift in economic strength that has taken place between SIA members and NSAA members, between the manufacturers and the resort operators. The resort owners are the current beneficiaries, but to the extent that this shift stifles equipment innovation, everyone loses. Long-term, suppliers need a stronger business model.

There are other changes worth noting. The number of specialty retailers continues to decline. A few decades ago, the traditional skier purchased hard-goods and softgoods in the early season, pre-Christmas. The industry-leading softgoods, parkas, shells, and pants were typically available only in those specialty ski shops. One purchased early, before the product was sold out. And in those bygone days, there was something of a passion for fashion and traditional ski-specific brands. That's changed … functionality now rules. Today, the clothing space is dominated by the big guys, The North Face, Patagonia, L.L. Bean, and the like, not by the brands we grew up with, such as Obermeyer, Descente, and Bogner.

TAKE VAIL RESORTS, which operates about 180 shops nationwide, as an example. Vail Resorts purchased half of Tom and Ken Gart's operation, Specialty Sports Venture (SSV), in the late 1990s. Vail Resorts rolled their existing resort shops into that division, with the stores branded to their location, i.e. Breckenridge Sports, Vail Sports, Heavenly Sports, and so on. About five years ago, Vail Resorts purchased the remaining 50 percent, and it is now the most powerful individual buyer in the SIA world. Vail Resorts is in a position to drive the best deals (lowering margins for the SIA manufacturers) while improving the profitability of its retail division.

This also puts into perspective the challenges SIA faces with its annual show. If Vail Resorts so desires, it could simply say to suppliers: "Meet us at our Keystone Convention Center in February. We'll place our orders there and won't be attending the Denver show."

THE SIA SHOW WAS THE CASH COW that for years defined the respective roles of NSAA and SIA. While it's still a major event, it faces increasing competition from the Outdoor Retailer show in Salt Lake City, and the declining strength of small, mom-and-pop stores nationwide, who are challenged to leave their shops and who can do their business at regional shows. And then there's the predictable, annual argument about timing. Decades ago, the SIA Show occurred in March. This was a time that worked for specialty retailers. By then, each knew or should have known their "open to buy," and there were discount incentives offered to actually write orders at the show.

As more and more softgoods were being produced in China, the timing for order placement changed. In order to secure production slots, apparel commitments had to be made by the clothing distributors much earlier in the season. This led to the current January timetable for the Denver show, and the mantra of "See it, Try it, Buy it," which actually only applies to hardgoods and accessories, not the softgoods that have an earlier order deadline. In spring 2016, the SIA board voted to move the show date to December with the hopes of appealing to the large softgoods companies. There was such a hue and cry that the decision was reversed, and the show date reverted back to January.

SIA has hired a new president following the retirement of longtime leader David Ingemie. In the summer of 2016, the new leadership began the process of closing down the McLean office, terminating the vast majority of staff, and relocating to Park City. One possible show option is a merger with the producers of the Outdoor Retailer Show to offer two shows, one focused on hardgoods (January in Denver) and the other of softgoods (earlier, in the fall, in Salt Lake).

HOW TIMES HAVE CHANGED since the USIA debacle! The resorts have become the clear winners and innovators in the 21st century, while the suppliers have suffered market setbacks and numerous issues, some their own fault but many just a result of disruptive market forces, such as online sales.

While SIA research indicates that total industry sales revenue has mostly pointed upward over the decades, there was a major shift of dollars in the late 1990s to the snowboard industry, away from glamorous, once-powerful alpine hardgoods suppliers, who are now selling fewer units than at any time in recent history. There has been a helpful boost from new products, such as helmets and POV cameras, but that gain has been more than offset by a continued dominance by non-ski-specific apparel, the North Faces and Patagonias, who aren't part of the SIA family and don't even exhibit at the SIA show.

Over the years, SIA's mission has focused almost solely on the cash cow that was the SIA show. The member-owned trade association generated considerable cash flow from the show, and also has a robust "rainy day fund" set aside. But the result of the increased emphasis on the show was that suppliers spent more and more money to fight each other for a smaller piece of an ever-shrinking pie.

IN MANY WAYS, NSAA and SIA reflected the personalities and styles of their leaders, both of whom are passionate, knowledgeable, dedicated professionals in their own ways. There is a bit of a "tortoise and the hare" analogy here. David Ingemie typically put himself out front in the public, in the press, always speaking to show-related issues, and looking for bold ways to help the sport. Michael Berry preferred to stay patiently in the background, guiding thoughtful research and analyzing the necessary next steps (see the "Model for Growth"). Berry shaped big-picture policy and and provided advice, inspiration, and support to move the resorts forward in a slow but steady and politically savvy manner. One might say the turtle won, or is at least winning. But the sport needs both to be successful. If SIA moves forward with the OR merger, perhaps the organization will have the energy and time to focus on issues that are arguably more important to the long-term health of the industry than the annual show.

CHAPTER 14

So, Do You Really Get to Ski All the Time?

(And What Do You Do in the Summer?)

Well, no. Let's just say that I get to spend a lot more time skiing now that I'm retired. Last winter, I skied almost 70 days at Steamboat. Not bad considering the number of days we were travelling out of town. I also managed to hit Copper, A-Basin, and Vail.

Skiing in retirement is a totally different experience from that of skiing while managing a resort. In the latter case, I would be alert to any lift-related issues, the condition of load and unload ramps, signage, and the quality of grooming. Was each staff member attentive, and greeting the guests with a smile and with enthusiasm?

I would try to ride as many different lifts as possible, depending on the amount of time I had. As managers, we all have strengths and weaknesses. One of my attributes was attention to detail. There was a game we played as kids: "What's wrong with this picture?" The idea was to recognize what was missing or out of order from one picture to the next, ostensibly a duplicate. I was very good at that. Seeing what was wrong was definitely a skill I brought to the job as an area manager. It was also a weakness if I let that dominate my communication with staff. If you're constantly pointing out what is wrong, you quickly wear out your welcome. "Oh, here he comes again..."

That lesson was learned over time, so I would make the mental notes relative to any issues and wait until the right moment (unless it was an immediate safety issue) to bring it up to the appropriate manager. Fundamentally, any correction or criticism had to be positive. Focus on what was right, and then mention what could have been done differently to make it better.

The ski business is a service business. Service starts with the staff. If employees don't treat each other with respect and provide great "service" to each other, how can we expect our staff to have a quality interaction with guests? So skiing around was a process of collecting and organizing the information that would allow us to do a better job, every day, every season. While getting outside in the wondrous winter environment that was my workplace was always great, it was not relaxing. This was my vocation, and it required focus and discipline. Not the same as heading off for first tracks in retirement.

The reality is that much of the job of running a ski area takes place in an office or meeting room. The challenge is to find a balance between the "managing" part of the job and actually immersing yourself in the resort experience. That means skiing. It also means observing the resort as the guest does.

My routine in Steamboat wasn't much different from my Vermont protocol. As many days as possible, I would try to walk the "path" that the guest would take. Starting in the parking areas, the drop-off areas, the ticket windows, and into the base lodges. Taking time to pick up trash, if needed. Just showing that I cared about the little things. In Steamboat, I would often cross paths with Mike Circle, our Ambassador Supervisor, as he wandered through Gondola Square, our base area, making sure that all was in order for the day. That often included repositioning our ubiquitous red wagons, used to transport skis, boards, and small children from the transportation center to the slopes. Walking through the base area also provided for interactions with guests and staff. I've heard it called MBWA, management by wandering around. Highly recommended!

AT MOUNT SNOW, I had a regular weekend routine that I shared with my longtime friend, Dr. Harry Haroutunian. Harry was one of two local docs, meaning he had to deal with most of the medical problems of residents in our area of Windham County, principally West Dover and Wilmington. Considering it was rural Vermont, he was also the medical examiner. And if that didn't keep him busy enough, he operated the triage center at the base of the ski mountain, named after its founder, the legendary Dr. Mickey Wolf. Mount Snow was 45 minutes to an hour from the nearest hospital, so most serious injuries had to be dealt with on-site.

Mickey had an X-ray machine, and in the "good old days" of "bear trap" and cable bindings, he was known to have set more than 30 broken legs on a busy day. There were only a handful of beds for use by skiers waiting to see Mickey, so some days the injured simply waited outside, securely strapped in their ski patrol sleds, until the doctor could see them. By the time Mickey had passed on and Dr. Harry took over, there were significant improvements in release bindings and the injury rate had declined dramatically. But there were always injuries. Let's just say that the center was a busy spot on any weekend or holiday.

There was a "quiet" period for Harry early in the morning, so we would head out as soon as the lifts opened on Saturday and Sunday. We had a routine that would make sense to any avid Mount Snow skier. We'd head up the Canyon lift (No. 9). One run off that lift, then back up, down River Run to the North Face. One run over there, and then back to the top. Down the Sunbrook to Bear Trap lift, then over to Carinthia. A short visit in the Lodge, and then we'd ride the Carinthia lift and work our way over to Sundance. Visiting each lodge on the way. Checking out how the morning developed as the crowd began arriving. Eventually, we would return to the main base area, around 10 a.m., and go our separate ways, each dealing with the crises that each day seemed to provide. This we did in all sorts of weather: bluebird days, sub zero, rain or freezing rain, even snow. Remember, this was New England. If you don't like the weather, just wait a minute.

ON WEEKENDS AND HOLIDAYS AT MOUNT SNOW, my children, Keenen and Elizabeth, would head to the mountain with me first thing. My job was to get them to their lesson programs. They would swing by my office at various times during the day, which was just great. And I would catch them visiting with Rena LaMarche, our extraordinary baker, who fed them more than their fair share of cinammon buns.

Sometimes, at the end of the day, I could sneak in a run with them. They were a constant presence in my ski life when they were preteens. Then, the more formal race obligations came along, and they would be travelling as many days as they trained at Mount Snow. Because I made several trips to other resorts over the course of a typical winter, I always tried to bring one of them whenever possible. I remember bringing Elizabeth with me to Park City at age 5 for an NSAA Winter Show (it was 1987, the year the New York Giants beat the Denver Broncos in the Super Bowl). I put her in Ski School and then caught up with her for a few runs at the end of the day. After the show, we spent a few deep powder days at Snowbird. When we got back to Vermont, Elizabeth announced to the family that she "wasn't skiing in Vermont anymore!" I think that was only partially due to her first experience out West. She didn't get along with her coach ... but after a few weeks in solitary, she got back to skiing Mount Snow.

Many years later, I was able to take the whole family on a CMH heli-skiing trip. We stayed in Revelstoke, because Eileen has a "thing" about riding helicopters, and she could ski at the new resort there, which was being run by a former Vermonter, Rod Kessler, who had put in many years at Killington and Stowe.

For the kids and me, the weather was near perfect and the skiing spectacular. For those who haven't experienced heli-skiing, put it on your bucket list. When the weather is good (there are some snowy/cloudy days when you're restricted to skiing in the trees), there's nothing like it. You ski above tree line in untracked terrain so vast it's almost unimaginable. We were there in early April, so the weather was warming and we could hear huge spring slides letting loose in adjacent drainages. Just a low rumble and reminder that our snow surface was beginning to settle.

On our last day, the guide commented, "Listen, I know where the crevasses are [only an experienced eye could pick out where they would be opening], so I want you to follow me closely, not in my line but just adjacent. Do not stop until I stop." Off he went, and we followed over 1,000 feet of vertical, came to a little rise, and there he was, just a speck in the distance. So we continued, legs burning. When we finally stopped, we'd covered several thousand vertical feet, and the whole group just about collapsed. He wryly noted, "I just couldn't find a safe place to stop!"

NOW FAST FORWARD TO MY RETIREMENT. Almost every day that I was in town for the winter of 2015–16, it was off to ski for First Tracks at 8 a.m., or shortly thereafter (the perks of being the ex-boss). I had two regular skiing partners, Loris Werner, and my wife, Eileen. Unfortunately for Eileen, on December 3, a bluebird Steamboat day, we were heading down Buddy's Run in a small group that included Rob Perlman, Steamboat's new president, and John Kohnke, the ski-patrol director. Just a few turns down the run, Eileen crashed and broke her collarbone. It was early in the day with hardly anyone on the slopes yet. And she was in good company, if there had to be an accident. I don't think it's possible to be much farther away from the base first aid, so she had a long ride by toboggan from just below the top of Storm Peak to the base. We joked that she got her money's worth. Then off to the emergency room and, eventually, surgery late that afternoon. We now have matching titanium plates in our right collarbones (mine, thanks to a crash in Courchevel, France, on a visit some six years ago).

It's a reality of the sport that sometimes you get hurt. If so, as we were reminded that day, the quality of medical care in mountain towns like Steamboat is astounding. From initial assessment and transport by ski patrol, to the competent, patient-friendly care in the emergency room, this negative experience could not have been better handled. Once the diagnosis was confirmed, the ER staff suggested that we talk to a doctor about treatment options. We met with Dr. Andreas Sauerbrey, who recommended surgery given the nature of her break. Andreas does over a hundred similar surgeries each year. That's what you want to hear when considering whether or not to take that approach. Andreas adjusted his schedule so that she could have surgery late that afternoon. By 7 p.m. she was home, resting comfortably. Thank you, Steamboat Ski Patrol and Yampa Valley Medical Center.

Bad news for Eileen. She was out of action for at least a month. The good news for me was that Loris (aka "Bugs") Werner became my ski partner. Bugs is the youngest sibling of the famous Werner skiing family, and spent many years on the U.S. Ski Team with brother, Buddy, arguably the greatest American skier at the time, and his sister, Skeeter, also an Olympian in alpine skiing. Skeeter, as attractive as she was athletic, had graced the cover of *Sports Illustrated*. She married Doak Walker, the legendary Heisman Trophy winner (SMU) and NFL star, and the two were as close to royalty as you could find in Steamboat. Sadly, Loris' family members had all passed away: Buddy died in an avalanche near St. Moritz, Switzerland, while filming with Willy Bogner in spring 1964, and Skeeter succumbed to cancer in 2001, while a patient at the Doak Walker Care Center in Steamboat.

Loris' mother, Hazie, was a legend in Steamboat Springs for her hospitality and genuine friendliness, often inviting strangers into her home over the holidays. When she would hear locals complaining about the "newcomers" to town, she was known to remark, "Well, we let *you* in, didn't we?" Everyone knew the Werner family. Remember, it *is* called Mt. Werner, and the library *is* the Buddy Werner Memorial Library.

I had known Loris for many years. He's married to our Lift Manager, Deb Werner, and we often met for company Christmas parties and such. And he often made presentations at our annual staff orientations, talking about the history of skiing in Steamboat. Loris could easily be mistaken for a rodeo cowboy ... not an ounce of fat, and the kind of rancher demeanor that says "hard work and no foolin' around." Following his ski-racing career, he settled into various management roles at the ski area, including ski-school director and mountain manager. I couldn't have picked a better skiing partner. First, he was an incredible skier, and, second, he just had such great history to share.

I had been in Steamboat for 17 seasons, and thought I knew the mountain pretty well. But not the way Loris did. Our ski day would feature a mix of blues and blacks, Steamboat's legendary trees, but always gravitating to favorite runs at some point: Flintlock, Two O'Clock, Storm Peak to Sunset to Rainbow ... and anything at Pioneer Ridge, if the snow was good.

By 10:30, it would be time for a break. So off to Four Points lodge for coffee and, sometimes, a fresh, warm cinnamon bun. We would inevitably run into other skiing friends, share stories of the day's discoveries ... all in all, it doesn't get much better. After the break, we'd work our way down, typically done for the day before noon.

By February, Eileen was back skiing most days, so we became a threesome and, some days, a foursome when former Steamboat President Hans Geier would join us. One day while riding the Storm Peak Lift, Loris was talking about growing up as a kid in Steamboat and how he, Buddy, and Skeeter would put on skis at home in downtown Steamboat, shuffle out to the street, and just grab on to the bumper of the first passing car ... and ride it as close to Howelsen Hill as they could get. So began their day of race training. The roads were all snow covered; there were no paved roads downtown. Eileen said: "Bugs, you have to write this down!" He agreed, and I signed on to help him. That will be fun.

"WHAT DO WE DO IN THE SUMMER?" Well, it's work. Budgets for the following year have to be prepared. Operations shift to maintenance and construction. Depending on the scope of the capital program, this can be a major effort.

But in the "old" days, if summer did not bring a major project, it was quiet. Summer operations were basically running a chairlift or gondola for sightseers. This was before mountain biking, zip lines, big-time weddings, etc. By way of perspective, in today's Steamboat, virtually any summer weekend brings as many guests to town as a peak winter holiday. They are not here for as long and don't spend as much, but the energy is palpable. If you're in management at Steamboat, you're on call every weekend.

Killington in 1974 was different ... very quiet. So I had an opportunity to chase my dream: learning how to sail. I bought a boat on Lake George with my friend Barron Clancy. Marty Wilson, who got me hooked in the first place, came over on weekends and taught us how to race the boat, an old, fixed-keel, Bristol 22. We had a blast. The next boat was larger, a C&C 25, and we won three consecutive Lake George Corinthian Club championships. That was the beginning of a wonderful racing career.

My boss, Pres Smith, was a passionate sailor. He kept an Alden Sloop on Lake Champlain, and then moved up to a Tartan 41 (called Wildfire), berthed in Newport, Rhode Island. We did our first Bermuda Race on that boat in 1978. Pres then moved up to a C&C 43 (Aragon), and we did Bermuda in 1980. By that time, we had a group of friends/crew members who wanted to go to the next level in offshore racing. So we formed a syndicate and bought a C&C 40 (Coyote).

The 40 class, at the time, was highly competitive, so we were tiptoeing into the higher levels of ocean racing. In those days, my family was kind enough to basically let dad go racing every weekend from the end of April until July, when we settled into Lake George for the summer. Eileen's mom still lived in Nyack, New York, so we would often stay there on weekends when the racing was focused on Long Island Sound. We had a successful Block Island Race Week that first year with Coyote and won numerous races on the East Coast circuit.

Eventually, we sold Coyote to a group that had leased it for the 1982 Bermuda Race. That was a turning point for me. Rather than writing checks to sail and being a partner/owner, I had become part of a crew that would stick together for almost 15 years, going from boat to boat, typically following the lead of the professionals at North Sails East—the Milford, Connecticut, loft where the likes of John Marshall, Jim Crane, Andreas Josenhans, and others had their offices.

I learned three lessons from those years that were incredibly helpful in allowing me to manage through difficult circumstances ... not to mention enriching my life experience. Sailing and skiing share a lot in common.

The first was sailing with Michael Levin on Bright Finish, a 42-foot, Peterson-designed racing machine, built at Newport (RI) Offshore under the direction of Kim Roberts, who often crewed with us. Newport Offshore was a highly respected boatbuilder at the time, having delilvered several aluminum 12-meter contenders. Michael was Harvard-educated right down to the MBA, and running the Titan Industrial Corporation, a large steel-trading and manufacturing company that was family owned. He had been a mountain climber, polo player, and extreme skier, but had never sailed. He decided to learn the offshore racing game, and set his sights on winning the Admiral's Cup, the Super Bowl of sailboat racing. To make a long story short, he did not succeed, but he came incredibly close.

Michael was a great leader and organizer. He created a culture that by its very brashness (winning at the highest level) attracted a talented group. He left sailing after the failed Admiral's Cup effort, threw himself into polo, and never looked back. In October 2014, we held a reunion of the crew in Steamboat, and incredibly, virtually everyone showed. We shared some memories that night but mostly talked about how the experience of striving for excellence had affected everyone in their own careers. Thanks to Michael for showing all of us how to set goals and organize to achieve them.

One of the professionals who sailed on many of our boats was John Marshall, a veteran of multiple America's Cup campaigns, bronze medalist in the Dragon Class at the 1972 Olympics, and an executive with North Sails. Marshall's lessons to all who sailed with him: preparation and intensity. Need I mention that he was very smart? A Harvard grad with a major in nuclear physics.

I remember arriving in Newport for another Bermuda Race, this time on a Peterson 55 (Elusive). Marshall was surveying the boat the day before the departure, and hours before the "measuring," I heard him say: "What is this, a floating furniture factory?"

For hours, we removed every piece of furniture we could from down below, leaving a spartan galley and bunks. The owner looked on, a bit bewildered, as John was taking his boat apart. Marshall's comment: "This is a sailboat race, not a cruise." We would be much faster with these changes. The next morning, as the crew boarded, he would inspect all carry-ons, limiting the amount of weight that any crew member could bring aboard.

Once racing, John's intensity was legendary. Most skippers (in those days) would call for a headsail change (up or down in terms of size) when the wind changed in a material way. Marshall would call for a change any time he felt there was an advantage to be gained. Middle of the night. Time after time. He would exhaust the crew, but as a crew member, you were confident that we was striving for perfection, whatever the circumstances.

He had only one weakness, seasickness, but he never let that affect his role on the crew. In the middle of an awful Gulf Stream storm (we had blown through three headsails), I was on the foredeck trying to fix a loose leech cord when Marshall tossed his lunch to leeward. At that moment, given his distraction, we speared a big wave. The owner, John Edelman, was trying to help us with the jib and holding on to the jackstay. The sudden lurch of the boat threw him on to me. We both went overboard with Edelman, a big man, on top of me. Fortunately, I was connected to the rail with my harness and my right leg was wrapped around the lifelines. The whole bow went under, and as it rose, John Edelman was still on top of me. It was a painful moment, hanging upside down. I think it was Walt Levering who pulled John off me and then pulled me back on board. Everything settled down, and nothing more was said. Just another race with John Marshall. I can't remember if we won, but surely we were in the top echelon of boats in our class.

My third story is a brief one. In the late 1980s, we wound up sailing with Bruce MacLeod, first on his one-tonner, Sky Hie, and then on a J-35 of the same name. We went all over the place: Chicago, San Francisco . . . to wherever high-level regattas were being held.

The first time I sailed with Bruce, it was the Sardinia Cup Trials in Newport. It was late May and cold, very cold, especially the water temperature that time of year. Before the race starts, someone has to go overboard and "band the prop." This is a simple maneuver that ensures the prop won't open while sailing, causing unwanted drag. There was a paid crew member and any number of guys who could have sucked it up and done this. Bruce never asked anyone . . . he just stripped to his jockey shorts and went overboard into the frigid water.

That's leadership by example. He was arguably the most consistent "winning skipper" of all the guys I raced with. He was incredibly competent (having started as a one-design, small-boat sailor), but he inspired all who sailed with him. So the crew always put in the extra effort for Bruce. The best crews always wanted to be on his team. Is it a surprise that he was a consistent winner?

.I was one lucky ski-area manager to have this "other life."

CHAPTER 15

State of the Industry:

Look How Far We've Come

To this point, I've been looking backwards . . . way back, in some cases, to a very different time. But throughout those 40-plus years, one thing has remained constant: the enduring appeal of skiing (and riding). With that reality, being able to work in a business that draws its breath from the sport has been incredibly satisfying.

So what about the future? Good? Bad? Different?

First of all, the sport has never been more affordable, *if* one is willing to put up dollars in advance of the season and take the risk of not skiing/riding the expected number of days (and if you patronize the resorts that compete in the discounted season-pass markets, more on that later). The repricing of the lift ticket is the most positive consumer-marketing change I've seen in my career, and arguably the one with the most positive impact on the business. The flip side: if you show up on the spur of the moment at one of the large resorts that employs a dynamic pricing model, be prepared for sticker shock. It will be just like making a last-minute airline reservation. No deals available. Sorry.

The current pricing model will probably remain in place as long as the total number of participants is growing, even slowly, and the number of days skied or ridden remains higher than historic norms. Despite fears that

Millennials might not embrace the ski/ride lifestyle with the same passion as Boomers (the other comparably large generation), they appear to have leapt in. The sport remains highly aspirational. There is no comparable success story if you look at participation sports over a multidecade period. Golf has struggled for years against declining participation and just recently appears to be moving the needle in the right direction. Golf is very different. No one wears a GoPro when playing golf. For Millennials and younger, skiing and riding is a process of constant personal recording and sharing. The images are everywhere. Skiing. Snowboarding. They're cool.

For older Boomers enjoying senior pricing, they've been able to hang on and participate at a level that would have been unheard of 20 years ago. While many grumble about recent price increases, the senior pass is still a good deal. And generally, this group has the ability to pay!

Most of the early-morning participants I see at Steamboat are in their 60s or older. These Boomers are in incredible physical shape, and they are having a blast. Slower, yes, but still accomplished. By 11:30, the ski day is pretty well over, but not before they've had their midmorning break and still enjoyed the equivalent of a full-day's skiing by historic standards. Detachable lifts and Steamboat's "champagne powder snow" allow us Boomers to pack in huge vertical in just a few hours. Best news: there's still the rest of the day to be enjoyed.

The equipment now available is partially responsible; the gear and apparel companies deserve praise for continuously innovating. Shorter, wider skis provide a stable platform for a variety of conditions. Waterproof, breathable clothing, worn in "layers," means cold weather isn't a deterrent. If your hands get cold, you can invest in heated gloves. Same for ski boots. Every aspect of the sport, from an equipment perspective, has improved dramatically. One result is that many of the early impediments to skiing/riding have been removed or dimished. A second is that aging participants are able to stay active well beyond normal ski "retirement" age.

If the changes in gear are dramatic, they pale in light of the modern on-mountain ski/ride experience. In my judgment, the most dramatic impact is new snowmaking technology. In the older snowmaking systems, a moisture-laden end product was the result of an expensive, energy-intensive process of mixing warm, compressed air with water. Today, while this mixing is still an essential part of the process, snowmaking "guns" are typically tower-mounted, 10- to 30-feet above the slope, and issue a quiet, energy-efficient stream of dry snow. The ratio of compressed air to gallons of water produced has dropped dramatically, requiring a much smaller investment in compressed-air equipment and significantly lowering energy costs. And, most importantly, the product is better, dramatically better. With drier snow, it just means less "boilerplate," also known as Eastern ice. Skiers and riders might not even consciously know of the great surface improvement, but I can tell you as an operator that they have come to expect it.

The important ingredient now is water. Ski areas that have the ability to pump large volumes of water can take advantage of cold snaps to make snow when it's most efficient. This is also a huge hedge against the impacts of climate change, with many areas of the country experiencing warmer winters. The nonwinter of 2015–16 back in the East is the current classic example. While this was a devastating season for many resorts, it might well have been "terminal" absent modern snowmaking. Unlike water used for irrigation or public consumption, snowmaking is largely a noncomsumptive use. Area operators are essentialy "storing" snow on the slopes for a return to local streams and rivers later in the spring.

After snowmaking, the next most significant improvement is the transition to high-speed, detachable lifts from the older fixed-grip model. Old Warren Miller ski films often included a segment that focused on the unloading platform of an older double chairlift. Many of these scenes were shot in Southern California, where there's typically a higher percentage of new versus experienced skiers. For several minutes, the film captures, on fast-forward, the continuing pileup of new skiers attempting to unload the lift. The lift operator, at one point, in total frustration, starts throwing skis off the ramp as he drags the fallen guests out of the way ("Want your skis? Go get 'em," intones Warren). The lift keeps on running until there's no exit path on the ramp. The lift stops. The audience is hysterical, no matter how many times they've seen this. It's only funny because we, as skiers and riders, have experienced something like this at one point or another. We're laughing at our own memories as much as the poor initiates crashing in the film. Even for accomplished participants, sometimes getting "uphill" has been more challenging than going "downhill."

Enter the detachable chairlift. The chair that you ride "detaches" from the haul cable for the lift and transfers to a conveyor moving at a slow speed. One just pushes forward to the loading point and sits down as the chair arrives. The conveyor speeds up, and the chair reattaches to the haul cable. This process is repeated at the unload station. With alert operators, there are virtually no mistakes with loads. The Warren Miller film company could set up cameras for a whole month and not record comparable wreckage. Not only are there fewer accidents, but the lifts seldom need to stop or slow down to address problems. Everyone benefits from this efficiency.

The amount of time spent sitting versus skiing or riding has been dramatically reduced. The newer lifts travel at over twice the speed of the older ones. The bottom line: one can ski at least twice the amount of vertical feet in a day as in the "good old days." For most participants, this means a shorter and more relaxed ski day . . . more time sitting on the deck of Four Points, just absorbing the wonder of being outside in a beautiful alpine environment. Of course, there are the few crazy-busy days, when lines can be long, but there's always a way to separate from the crowds. We go early and leave early if it's busy. The ski experience has never been as pleasurable, and much credit goes to the new lift technology.

If you started skiing in the 1960s or '70s, you probably remember the ubiquitous "ticket wicket" (invented at Killington). You placed a wire loop through your jacket zipper and had your day lift ticket stapled or glued around the wicket. So the morning went something like this:

✓ Follow slow-moving traffic into the parking lot;
✓ Try to find a spot as close as possible to the lodge;
✓ Put on cold boots while sitting half in/half out of the trunk (perhaps the day's worst experience);
✓ Walk clumsily to the ticket window, schlepping skis and poles;
✓ Wait in a long line to purchase the day ticket;
✓ Keep waiting in line because the ticket printer just broke down;
✓ Attach ticket to wicket;
✓ Head off to the ski lift;
✓ Wait in the liftline;
✓ Meet ticket checker, who informs you that the ticket is improperly attached;
✓ Go back to the ticket booth;
✓ Wait in line;

✓ Get new ticket, attach it properly to wicket;

✓ Return to the now 30-minute liftline and start your day.

I have vivid memories of this process taking more than two hours before getting in a single run.

Did I mention that before the wicket, the ticket was actually stapled to your jacket? Of course, these were the days before Gore-Tex. It was a badge of courage and commitment to have a thick wad of used tickets still stapled to your army-surplus jacket. Aaahhh. The good ol' days.

Contrast this experience to today's RFID chip-based "media." At many resorts, there is no paper "ticket." Instead, a pass is issued, usually with the holder's photograph, and loaded with your lift-ticket privileges. It's backed by a credit card and can be used for virtually all transactions at the resort (or in the case of conglomerates, any member resort). All payments can be handled online. Children can be issued a pass with a fixed amount of "charging capacity" included. The holder never has to return to the ticket office. With Vail Resorts' Epic Passes, there are a number of other enhancements, including the ability to scan the pass through your parka and earn "points" as credits against future purchases. The pass also ties into Epic Mix, which tracks lifts and vertical skied, regularly dispensing achievement badges.

What was once a signature, negative experience for participants is now a relationship-building process. The more one spends at a given resort, the more the resort knows about buying habits and can customize solutions. Amazon.com on skis.

THERE IS A DIFFERENCE between the haves and have-nots in this game. Some smaller resorts simply can't afford the latest technology, but more affordable solutions are available. One space where they probably can't play is in the expensive installation of "access gates." Many resorts have installed access gates in the lift mazes. The gate opens when an authorized pass is in proximity. There are still ticket checkers, but they stand back from the gates, and as each one opens, a picture of the guest appears on their computer.

So the guest hassle has been eliminated, but the resort still has sufficient security to ensure that passes are not being resold or shared. Each use is recorded, so the resort and guest know when and even where (if all lifts have access gates) the usage occurred.

In Steamboat, access agates were recently installed on the major lower-mountain and upper-mountain access lifts. One lift that is popular with families (particularly when they would rejoin at the end of the day when ski-school classes were released), is the Christie Peak Express, a detachable six-pack. Before gates were installed, parents and kids would have to remove their passes from under layers of clothing to present to the ticket checker. This is not an easy process, particularly with small children. Well, it's no longer a hassle. Vail Resorts' mountains introduced this scanning process for the 2008–09 season, and many of my old-school friends will say that of all the company's digital extensions around its Epic Mix tracking, the hassle-free scan remains the single greatest benefit of all.

WHAT CAN BE DONE ON THE MOUNTAIN with new grooming equipment is simply stunning. A few years ago, we experienced a poor snow year at Steamboat. That said, there was good cover and surface conditions were OK in most skiing areas. But some trails, either because of exposure or underlying terrain conditions, were presenting inconsistent skiing experiences.

One such trail was West Side, a popular black diamond. It does not have snowmaking, so the only way to improve the situation was to "move" snow from somewhere else to cover the bare or thin spots. Otherwise, we were looking at closing the trail. Above West Side is a large, flat area where the South Peak lift terminates. It receives very little traffic and had quite a bit of snow. I asked Davey Crisler, our slope-maintenance director, if it would be possible to move some of that snow down to West Side, a distance of more than 1,000 feet. His response was, basically, "We've never done that before, but we'll try." He had the advantage of several new "Beast" snowcats, the largest built to date. And to make a long story short, experienced operators were able to move enough snow over that distance to re-cover West Side. It was amazing.

Grooming equipment can do things to tired snow and ice that were inconceivable just a few years ago. Back in the East, where grooming works hand-in-hand with modern snowmaking plants, ski areas are able to recover from adverse weather events in just a matter of days. Generally, visitors enjoy a predictable, quality snow surface despite the fickleness of Mother Nature.

NO AREA OF THE EXPERIENCE needed reinventing more than the "rental shop." It was an early-industrial-era production line just a few decades ago. Now, the process is more personalized. Television monitors welcome the guest and explain the process. Boot heaters ensure that the guest is not stepping into the sweaty, wet boot that someone else rented the day before. Modern ski bindings are easily adjustable. And they work. Injuries from bindings that fail to release are almost unheard of. In fact, the binding manufacturers indemnify the rental-shop operators against such claims. In the "old" days, the equipment that wound up in rental shops was the cheapest available. To no one's surprise, it often hindered the learning process and overall enjoyment. The equipment was often poorly maintained, meaning that dull edges made it difficult to hold an edge on firm snow. And fresh wax? Almost unheard of in rental shops, despite the fact that almost nothing improves skiing enjoyment more than a fresh coat of the correct wax. A good skier would never step into a rental shop. You bought and brought your own gear.

Now, modern operators provide a variety of equipment relative to skill sets, so travellers really don't need to drag along their skis or boards, especially on long flights. The fact that airlines now charge extra for bulky equipment and second bags has caused a dramatic shift in the percentage of guests who now rent or "demo" at the resorts. In many cases that number is over half, which means the rental shop business is highly lucrative with robust margins.

It's also very competitive. Operators can bring equipment right to your rented house or condominium, providing in-room fitting for the whole family. This typically happens the night of arrival, so the whole rental-shop hassle (which used to follow the ticket-window crisis) has been avoided. For those who choose the rental shop on day one, the experience is greatly improved, although nothing beats the convenience of in-room service, especially for the large family.

WHEN LOOKING AT THE SKI EXPERIENCE from the perspective of 20 years ago, the other area than cried out for reengineering was the Learn to Ski/Ride (LTS/R) experience. The general standard at that time: large classes, inexperienced instructors, cheap equipment, and crowded teaching areas.

Killington had pioneered LTS, but then lost focus. Les Otten made a significant investment and was partially successful in changing the ski-school cultures at his resorts. No one over questioned if it was a priority for Les.

But the major shift in focus occurred, in my judgment, because the NSAA made improving the experience its priority. NSAA-generated research demonstrated that if the ski areas didn't improve their retention (keeping skiers and riders engaged in the sport *after* their initial experience), then the future was grim indeed. Research showed that 80 to 85 percent of "never-evers" were leaving the sport after the initial introductory experience.

Some forecasts projected a 30-percent-plus decline in participation as active skiers retired from the sport and were not replaced. That got everyone's attention. As operators, we were attracting people to the sport, but we were not providing an experience that would retain them.

Improvements quickly followed, such as designated teaching areas with "magic carpet" lifts . . . moving carpets that took away the intimidation of the first lift ride, even if it was a "detachable." Class sizes shrunk, allowing more attention to individual needs. In many ski-school cultures, there was an awareness that more accomplished instructors had to dedicate their time to beginner instruction, helping coach younger instructors and not just doing privates. After all, these were the private-lesson clients of the future.

Better equipment was provided by manufacturers, especially Head Skis, which carved out a major business niche with its products. The new venues, combined with better equipment and motivated instructors, altered the way folks entered the sport. Many top resorts were succeeding in changing their culture to intensely focus on the new skier/rider, making sure that first day and following days exceeded all expectations. Success came slowly but steadily, with the NSAA promoting success stories, establishing annual recognition awards, and constantly focusing awareness on the importance of LTS/R.

EARLY SKI CULTURE was all about the cafeteria line and the burger and fries. Period. Food was an afterthought to most early mountain managers, and generally an area where few had much expertise or interest. And the business was small enough so that hiring true F&B professionals was difficult to justify. The result: boring cafeteria lines staffed by equally bored staff and very boring food. Little variety beyond the basic staples . . . and the prices were predictably steep. It was just something you put up with as an aggravating but unavoidable part of the ski experience. The cafeteria lines at lunch were so long that resorts would promote: "Eat early; eat late; ski high noon."

I'm sure there were other examples of early success in F&B, but I can think of two that drove a transformation. First was Deer Valley. From day one, management made it clear that this was all about the food. Their investment in dining lodges was over the top compared to the rest of the industry, where historically, the lodges and associated F&B operations were considered a necessity but not a priority. Deer Valley made the day as much about hanging out in the lodge and enjoying the food as it was about the skiing. Instead of crowded decks and hastily assembled barbecues, Deer Valley staff set out lounge chairs on the snow and delivered great food and beverages. And this in Utah. Beautiful architecture, fantastic food, well-trained staff, and a totally relaxed environment. This was closer to a high-end resort in the Virgin Islands than your typical ski area.

Then there was 33,000-square-foot Two Elk lodge at Vail, built atop the famous Back Bowls. Vail F&B, until that time, had been unremarkable, characterized by the crowds and long lines scrambling for mediocre food at Mid-Vail. Vail was about the scale and variety of the ski experience ... and a fun base village. Two Elk followed the Deer Valley model, but on a larger scale. It proved that the modern, large-volume ski resort could transform the way it fed and entertained its guests while they weren't skiing and riding. They charged top dollar. No one complained, because the food was great and the location stunning. High-speed lifts and an aging, affluent clientele meant that guests had more time to spend inside. The dining experience now covered not just noon, but much of the day. This also changed the math. Resorts could now afford to invest more in these amenities with the confidence they would build business and a return.

Steamboat historically suffered from a shortage of on-mountain dining seats, as noted regularly by guests in their comments to management and in our daily RRC reports. While Steamboat was regularly ranked among the Top 10 in *SKI* Magazine's annual Reader Resort Rankings, this seating shortage was an issue that needed fixing. Just below the Storm Peak face, at an elevation of 9,716 feet, sat an old warming hut called Four Points. This was a quaint facility, but totally inadequate for the volume of skiers looking for a warm seat and good food in that area of the mountain.

When we were finally given the financial resources to begin addressing seating issues, Four Points was the priority. Our planning team then did something that was totally uncommon in the early days of on-mountain lodge construction. First, led by Jim Snyder, the company's F&B professional, we established the food concept and the basic menu, which would feature fresh, on-premise products whenever possible. Then the kitchen was designed. Then the building envelope that would support the dining experience. We also wanted to make this a day/night venue, so the facility would have to be designed in such a way that it could convert from a high-volume day lodge to an intimate, snowcat-accessed evening dining experience.

Four Points benefitted from a great location. The typical "snow cloud" line, where visibility is impacted, begins just above the lodge, meaning that a spectacular view is offered most days of the winter. Easily accessed from all the major lift pods, it begins to fill shortly before 10 a.m. as "first trackers" take their first break of the day. These early-morning visits provide the lodge with extended hours of productive operations compared with other similar facilities.

The food is predictably excellent and creative. The bar, which provides views of the Storm Peak face, is perfect for people-watching and normally fills by 11 a.m. More than a hundred Adirondack chairs are spread out (Deer Valley–style) on the snow edge. The building has a small deck with additional seats, an outdoor fireplace, and a permanent barbecue. It's a happening spot. The Four Points evening dining experience reinforced what to date had been a Steamboat plus: the variety of on-mountain fine dining (Ragnar's, Hazie's, etc.) while the new day lodge mitigated the negative of limited in-lodge seating. A huge home run, so popular that it already needs to be expanded.

Steamboat is not unique in its focus on the on-mountain dining experience. Winter Park constructed a similar facility, called Lunch Rock, and it was an instant success. Tour any of the major Rocky Mountain resorts, and both the quality of new buildings *and* the associated food are notable. For me, one of the great pleasures of checking out another ski area is enjoying the on-mountain dining experience. I'm seldom disappointed.

So, again: this is not your father's ski business. It's thoroughly modern, while the timeless, adrenaline-releasing excitement of the sport endures. The companies that operate America's ski resorts have evolved from largely lift companies to fully integrated resort operations, where every aspect of the ski experience is reviewed, analyzed, and improved as needed to provide a competitive experience. Those that drop behind the curve find their market share slipping in an accelerated fashion. That said, most get the picture, and despite all the sales of resorts, recombinations, conglomeration, and arrival of Epic-ness, most ski areas have maintained their appeal and provide a quality experience in all the areas noted above. Which explains why few areas have gone by the wayside and why one company, to date, has been unable to capture enough market share to dominate the industry.

STEPPING BACK FROM RESORT OPERATIONS for a moment, one of the other major changes since the early days has been the increasing appeal of "ski towns," a trend that began in earnest in the 1990s and shows no signs of slowing. They come in all shapes and sizes, remote rural communities like Steamboat Springs to semi-urban "super" towns like Breckenridge or Vail. What makes them different is that people want to live there. It's a quality of life that appeals to a certain population niche, one looking for an active lifestyle, an engaged public, cultural variety, diverse political views, and maybe most importantly, lots of young people.

While many rural communities suffer a steady exodus of population, most ski towns in the Rockies are growing, bucking the trend, expanding faster than the ski resorts attached to them. The advent of the internet has been a huge factor. In a place like Steamboat Springs, the internet makes up for many of the challenges of being nearly three hours from Denver and with limited air service (except winter). It's a surprisingly diverse economy: national headquarters for a large hedge fund, and home of Point6 socks, Smartwool, BAP and Big Agnes, multiple breweries, bicycle manufacturers like Moots and Eriksen, and a large contingent of investors and consultants who work remotely from Steamboat . . . and seldom miss a powder day. Not a bad lifestyle if you can arrange it. And many can.

This has transformed the community fabric from one basically anchored by ranching and skiing to one of amazing diversity. It includes a vibrant arts community, including the Strings Music Festival, one of Colorado's finest classical music venues. We are blessed with abundant water in Steamboat, as the Yampa River runs right through town. So now we have a paddleboard manufacturer. The list goes on. The young folks, here for the lifestyle, provide the energy behind these new businesses. We're fortunate to have a large group of retirees who have capital and are interested in investing in the local scene. I have one friend who has often repeated: "I want to invest in things I can see and touch every day."

What's happening in Steamboat is being repeated elsewhere in the mountain communities that are home to ski areas. A large number of outdoor gear and clothing manufacturers are setting up shop in (not so little now) Ogden,

Utah, minutes from great skiing at Snowbasin, and in nearby Park City. Again, lifestyle driven.

The East lacks some of the appeal of these Western communities, particularly when it comes to weather. Nonetheless, many are being discovered as appealing retirement options. Stowe comes to mind. Lake Placid in New York, home to the state-owned Whiteface ski area. North Conway and Woodstock, New Hampshire, with a number of resorts within a few minutes drive, are also vibrant, year-round communities.

Vermont is a tough place to do business. It has one of the highest tax rates in the nation, especially if you're a nonresident, second-home owner. The development approval process is costly and unpredictable. The population is shrinking, especially the all-important youth demographic. There are not many quality jobs once you get outside Burlington and its suburbs. Many of the ski towns languish in the off-season. There are exceptions, but drive Route 100 in June, along the spine of the Green Mountains, home to its ski resorts, and you'll find it's more than a little quiet. It verges on deserted and desperate. There will be some success stories, but I do think resorts in Vermont face an unusual and daunting challenge. It's unfortunate, since the state offers the best mountains and best access of all the New England ski options. I remember the comment: "Vermont would never have been so hard on its ski industry if the owners could have moved their mountains to New Hampshire." Time will tell.

CHAPTER 16

Dramatic Change:
Putting the Inc. in Ski Resorts

The ski-resort industry has undergone dramatic change over the 44 years that I was continuously involved. Ownership has shifted away from individual ski areas, with their cash-strapped but enthusiastic pioneers, who created new mountain experiences and, eventually, entirely new communities. It was not a place where money was made. Dick Bass, legendary owner of Snowbird, Utah, would often remark that "the best way to turn a large fortune into a small fortune was to own a ski area." Dick probably marveled at all the financial success stories he observed in the years that followed his proclamation in the 1960s. Some of the holding companies now are valued in the billions of dollars. It's a seller's market as I write, despite the more frequent weather catastrophies that attend global climate change. Resorts in strong markets with demonstrated profitability trade for 10 times EBITDA.

When I sat down in the fall of 2015 to begin this book, I knew the stories I wanted to tell and knew that I had enjoyed a unique perspective as I watched the business and sport change over the years. The process of writing, researching, and chasing down old colleagues for ideas brought clarity to where I think the business is headed.

First, since much of this book has covered the arrival and evolution (or self-destruction) of some of the mega-companies, where is that headed? Will there eventually be only a handful of conglomerates operating our ski areas?

I think not. While I have spent most of this book talking about the major players, one of the unexpected success stories in the ski business relates to small, urban ski areas. Small is a "relative" term. Wachusett Mountain, located an hour's drive from Boston, is one of the most popular and financially successful urban ski areas in the Northeast, perhaps the country. Owned by the creative and predictably unpredictable Crowley family, it is a veritable learn-to-ski factory. It operates day and night, with a constant stream of yellow buses discharging excited children. Its rental shops are some of the best run in the industry. It's facilities are up-to-date, the result of consistent, year-after-year reinvestment in the business. The Crowleys are passionate about the sport, and it shows, right down to what is one of the highest EBITDAs in the industry for a day ski area.

And they are not alone. Close to Washington, D.C., the Naylor family (Snow Time, Inc.) operates three highly successful ski areas. If you think the weather is unpredictable near Boston, think about being this far south.

Ski areas near major metropolitan areas, with effective snowmaking and solid management, will continue to prosper. Most of these have very engaged owners. Generally, the "For Sale" sign is not out. The ones interested in selling or needing to sell ... well, that's typically happened, or they've simply gone out of business.

Looking at the list of larger destination resorts that have not been acquired by the big guys, it strikes me that they are not only independent, but fiercely independent. Jackson Hole comes to mind. Jackson Hole isn't for sale. Telluride, owned by Los Angeles-based investor Chuck Horning, isn't for sale. Chuck has brought Bill Jensen in as a partner and manager. I suspect they're in Telluride for the long haul. Sun Valley was purchased in 1977 by the Earl Holding family, also owners of Snowbasin in Utah. This is the family that controls Sinclair Oil. Nope. I don't see them necessarily expanding their ski-area holdings, or selling them, either.

There have been "defensive" moves made in response to recent acquisitions by the biggest players. Deer Valley purchased nearby Solitude in order to defend its market share against Vail Resorts' Utah advance. Snowbird is now owned by Ian Cumming, principal of Powdr Corp., but he has not folded

Snowbird into Powdr and operates it independently. Mammoth Mountain purchased Bear Mountain and Snow Summit in Southern California. Vail Resorts controls Heavenly, Northstar and Kirkwood in the Lake Tahoe region. KSL added Alpine Meadows to its Squaw holdings. Under Mike Shannon and Eric Resnick, they are surely looking for additional properties. Mammoth's investment in Southern California needs to be looked at in the context of this new, competitive landscape.

Powdr recently closed on the purchase of Eldora, 35 minutes west of Boulder, Colorado. Having lost Park City to Vail Resorts, Powdr probably had cash, as well as the need to strengthen its hand in Colorado. Owning Eldora protects Copper in the event that, for whatever reason, Copper was dropped from the Rocky Mountain Super Pass suite.

Indeed, if you look at the recent transactions in the ski-resort business, most other than Vail Resorts' have been defensive. It's a bit like a chess game. We're almost at a stalemate … meaning, it's likely that the pace of mergers and acquisitions will slow considerably.

Some of the conglomerates, like St. Louis–based Peak, are loosely assembled collections of ski areas, lacking an obvious strategic purpose. Peak has avoided overbuilding its corporate office, so it will probably continue to acquire available, smaller resorts that might benefit from its snowmaking expertise. Other than that, since there's no evident strategic purpose, and considering the horrible 2015–16 winter west of the Mississippi, they might dispose of one or more areas if the price is right.

Intrawest. Well, I've suggested that at some point the parts may be worth more than the whole, unless they can add properties to better distribute holding company costs. Bill Jensen, the veteran operator who is as proficient and aggressive in acquisitions mode as anybody, couldn't consummate a deal before he left the company. Time will tell. The challenge for Intrawest, as well as any holding company, is right-sizing the corporate headquarters and spending relative to the collection of resorts. Importantly, it needs to be big enough to satisfy the reporting requirements of its ownership. That, of course, varies greatly if the owner is a private group, such as Powdr, or a public company. In the latter case, the financial team must be broadened to supply required SEC reporting and provide a responsive financial public-relations function. Beyond providing a level of financial detail that satisfies the needs of ownership, the holding company team needs to rigorously assess the cost/benefits of each position. Every position brings additional costs that subtract from the aggregate EBITDA of the operating companies.

The holding-company staff does not create income, it creates overhead. It is the nature of a company's headquarters group that it speaks to itself. Because it's physically remote from the ski areas, it's inevitable that the strongest relationships develop within the team. That's human nature. They work with each other day-in and day-out. They and their families socialize together. The drive to succeed translates into a desire to have more influence . . . and more staff.

Because there is only so much authority in any given organization, adding more to corporate means subtracting from the operating businesses. Only the best executives can stand up to the inevitable demands to grow corporate and find the right balance relative to the operating companies. In the case of ASC, the parts turned out to be worth more than the sum of the pieces. The Intrawest story isn't over. Whether ownership will realize the greatest value by continuing to operate a public company or finding a way to sell off the pieces, well, that's unknown. But I suspect it will be largely determined by the effectiveness and cost/benefit of the headquarters group. Most of the other holding companies are decentralized, with very small corporate offices (Powdr, Peaks, etc.). Vail Resorts is a different animal.

I mentioned earlier that, to date, no one conglomerate has been able to truly dominate the industry. That could change. If it does, it will be Vail Resorts. To understand how likely that is, one needs to look back into Vail's history, and then forward to its transformation under Rob Katz.

CHAPTER 17

Why Has Vail Resorts Been So Successful?

And Where Are They Headed?

M ention to someone in a packed Vail liftline today that the mega-resort's ownership once went bankrupt, and you'll get a strange look: "You gotta be kidding me."

Vail Associates, as it was known back then, went bankrupt in 1991 under George Gillett. The real-estate collapse and development costs from Vail's Beaver Creek project were a part of the challenge, though it was the owner's faltering broadcast business and his heavy reliance on junk bonds that ultimately brought the ski-resort operations down. But overall, the 1980s were not always kind to the ski business, even Vail, and Wall Street private equity, in this case Apollo Global Management, led by Leon Black, wound up with the assets.

Gillett is still fondly remembered by many as Vail's best owner, ushering in massive capital spending on new detachable lifts, focusing on service, and developing a very public presence on the mountain. Gillett had brought in a young financial wiz, Mike Shannon, to guide Vail and Beaver Creek through the 1980s, before leaving in 1992. I remember asking him at an NSAA Convention why he decided to depart. His answer: "I love the people in this business and its energy. It's hard to find anything quite like it. But I don't believe that skiing is a place where you can make a lot of money in the near term. Demographics are working against us. I'm focused on golf." (And so he was, by establishing a very successful private-equity firm, KSL Capital Partners, which over time cycled through many golf and hotel properties, buying and selling . . . successfully. Most recently, he returned to the ski-resort fold, purchasing Squaw Valley, and then adjacent Alpine Meadows. And as the circle closes . . . he hired Steamboat's marketing VP, Andy Wirth, to take the reins for the ski investments.)

I can also remember way back to when the Vail Resorts offices were located in downtown Avon, after Apollo had scooped up the assets left from the Gillett bankruptcy. This was during the Adam Aron and Andy Daly period. The HQ had moved from its offices in Lionshead to a weirdly modern structure called the Four Seasons, just west of the "main street" access road to Beaver Creek. It was called the "Dark Star" by locals and employees. The evil empire? I think not. But there was a sense, pervasive with guests and locals, that the parent Vail was a corporate monolith, disconnected from the realities of resort-community life, where decisions were being made thousands of miles away and with little concern for local impacts.

Vail Resorts had purchased Breckenridge and Keystone from Ralston Purina Corporation in 1997. It had also acquired Arapahoe Basin. And it owned Beaver Creek, which was now hitting its stride. Following review of the Ralston transaction from an antitrust perspective, Vail was forced to sell A-Basin, but could continue to offer joint pass products. This outcome was truly bizarre (and somewhat similar to Otten being forced to divest Cranmore and Waterville Valley). There was certainly more value in A-Basin's participation in joint marketing than there was in owning the small resort.

In terms of a ski-area holding company, Vail Resorts now had a unique advantage. Its four primary resorts were large by any metric. Only Beaver Creek did fewer than 1 million visits, but it was growing at a pace that exceeded industry norms. The resorts were physically close, which provided opportunities for shared services, especially on the marketing side. Management could easily visit each resort in a single day, providing significant command and control advantages compared to other ski holding companies. Vail Resorts controlled about 40 percent of total Colorado visits, but over 50 percent of all destination visits. No other company could match the marketing clout VR could bring to bear on this Colorado collection. Not to mention that all the resorts could be accessed from Denver International Airport or Eagle County Airport, ensuring reasonable but diverse air-travel options. And all sat along the busy I-70 corridor, a significant advantage when looking at the local, Front Range market.

LEON BLACK'S APOLLO GLOBAL MANAGMENT had assigned a young executive, Rob Katz, to the Vail account in 1992, and he had been intimately involved in the company's significant moves, including the purchases of Breckenridge, Keystone, and also Heavenly, and the RockResorts lodging outfit. He also had his hand on the wheel when Vail Resorts went public in 1997.

While in his 30s at the time, he had completed a number of high-profile deals and was perceived as a rising star. While nothing over time could diminish his obvious talents, there was a perception in ski circles that he was a "favored child." Following 9/11, Katz had left Apollo and New York City and moved his family to Boulder, though he stayed on as a lead board member for Vail Resorts. Following Adam Aron's departure, Katz assumed the reins as Vail Resorts CEO in February 2006.

Katz immediately moved Vail Resorts' HQ from the "Dark Star" to Broomfield, Colorado, much closer to DIA and to his home in Boulder. This was a significantly bigger relocation than the one from Vail to Avon, and it was only the beginning of things to come.

VAIL RESORTS IS NOW A DARLING ON WALL STREET. On August 15, 2016, in the wake of Katz's biggest deal to date, the purchase of Whistler Blackcomb in British Columbia, its stock closed at $153.53. That is a stunning fourfold-plus increase since Katz took over in 2006. Under Katz, the company acquired Northstar and Kirkwood to go with Heavenly in the Lake Tahoe region; Park City and The Canyons in Utah; three Midwest metro feeder areas, and Perisher in Australia, the Southern Hemisphere's largest ski resort. Vail Resorts is the worldwide leader in the ski industry.

How did this happen when so many ski stories have had sad or bad endings? Think of the American Skiing Company implosion or the shrinking of Intrawest.

First, its leader, Rob Katz. If ASC was undone by its CEO, Les Otten, Vail Resorts was successfully reengineered by Rob Katz as the premier ski-resort operator of winter destination resorts in the world. That's my opinion, but I don't know how it could be challenged. While there are ski resorts in Europe (such as Les Trois Vallées in France) that contain as many lifts as the entire state of Colorado, the ownership is fractured. They do not operate as integrated businesses (managing all the diverse revenue centers from lodging to restaurants, ski school, and rental/retail). Quite simply, in 2016, there is nothing globally to match the geographic scale, total skier visits, or financial performance of Vail Resorts. When Rob Katz arrived on the ski scene, the industry had never seen anyone like him. He didn't care what people thought of him. He was not fazed by the reaction to unpopular decisions. He just dragged the organization along, executing his vision, and along the way, created an economic juggernaut.

There might have been others who could have done well with the quality assets that Vail Resorts held and its dominant market share in Colorado. But to take the company forward—through acquisition, business refinement, and disciplined cost management—Katz has unquestionably overachieved. It's easy now to forget Katz's steering of the ship through the Great Recession, when he implemented necessary cutbacks, and even cut his own salary to $1 a year, or when he got out in front of a safety issue, requiring all Vail Resorts on-mountain staff to wear helmets.

Katz brought with him Wall Street savvy, an ability to manage up to his owners and shareholders, and just enough empathy and intuitive understanding of the resorts' communities that he could drive change without destructive resistance. He hasn't made serious tactical or strategic mistakes, showing a willingness to back off when required, such as with the company's withdrawal in the summer of 2016 of its controversial plan to trademark the name "Park City." Over his tenure, there haven't been a lot of costly political mistakes.

I can think of one. It's worth telling to provide a perspective on Rob Katz, but it may leave the reader as confused as I. In either event, it reflects the state of the ski business in Colorado.

In 2008, I was serving as chairman of Colorado Ski Country USA (CSCUSA), our state's trade association representing the 23 member ski areas. CSCUSA was a well-respected advocate for skiing in Colorado and enjoyed a national reputation as a well-run, member-focused trade organization. It was certainly the strongest of similar state associations in the U.S. and the one with the largest annual budget.

Our president was Rob Perlman, a young executive with experience within the Vail Resorts and Mammoth organizations. Rob had been hired to take the place of David Perry, who had left CSCUSA for a senior marketing position at Aspen Skiing Company. To many within the industry, the president's post was viewed as a stepping stone to a choice executive position at a resort somewhere in the state.

CSCUSA had a solid track record managing political and regulatory issues, thanks largely to the competence of Melanie Mills, the in-house attorney and trade-association lobbyist. Programs on the marketing side were not always as successful. I remember a hugely flawed ($1 million) initiative to drive visitation from Kansas (of all places). At least it was a lesson learned. This was back in the days when there was some residual belief that saturation marketing could build demand. This was pre-Internet, pre–social media, pre-everything!

So the association tended to look at marketing in a very pragmatic way by the mid-2000s. That said, we were getting feedback from John Garnsey, a CSCUSA board member and copresident of Vail Resorts' mountain resort division, that his company did not support the level of marketing currently being executed at CSCUSA. The comment, as John Garnsey reported to us, was that "Rob doesn't feel that Vail should be spending its money (via CSCUSA dues) helping its competitors be successful."

After much discussion among board members, it was agreed that CSCUSA would dramatically reduce the scope and cost of its marketing efforts. This had the impact of virtually "halving" everyone's dues, including Vail Resorts', which, it should be noted, was supplying more than a third of the association's dues, which were calculated by skier visits.

To thicken the plot, I had been negotiating with Rob Perlman to move to Steamboat and assume the role of VP of marketing. Andy Wirth, our longtime marketing lead, had been promoted to senior VP of marketing for Intrawest and was relocating to Vancouver. We had a big hole to fill at Steamboat. Rob was the guy we wanted, and he agreed to make the move. This was all happening while the negotiations with Vail Resorts regarding Colorado Ski Country were taking place. I didn't want to be perceived as double dealing, given my ongoing talks with Rob, so Mike Kaplan, Aspen's CEO, had taken the lead with the Vail Resorts negotiations.

At a board meeting in the late spring of 2008, in Edwards, Colorado, Vail Resorts representatives participated via conference call. The board reviewed and adopted the budget with all changes proposed by Vail Resorts now incorporated (timing was critical, as the Ski Country annual meeting was scheduled for the following week, and we would need a budget to propose).

The crisis seemed to have been averted. Ski Country would move on as the voice of skiing in Colorado, absent material marketing. I should clarify that many member resorts did not agree with the limited marketing strategy (especially the smaller resorts), but went along in order to accommodate Vail Resorts.

Once the budget was approved, I announced to the board that Rob Perlman had agreed to accept a position at Steamboat. I don't think there was anyone in the room who felt that it was anything other than a great move for Rob. After all, he was a marketing guy at heart, Ski Country was no longer doing any marketing, and it was time for him to move on.

Five minutes after the announcement, the call came in from Vail. "Rob says this announcement changes everything, Vail Resorts is out of Ski Country." Period. No further comment or discussion.

Wow.

Some years later, I was sitting in the lobby of the Steamboat Grand and talking to Governor John Hickenlooper about ski-business issues. I told the story about Vail Resorts' exit from Ski Country and asked if he had any ideas about why it had happened and how to get them back in the fold. I believed then and do now that Colorado should speak with one voice on industry issues. He leaned back and said, "I think you surprised him."

OK. Ski Country has moved on under the capable leadership of Melanie Mills. Rob Perlman now serves as president of Steamboat. There's a kind of strange balance of power in Colorado skiing. Ski Country and Vail Resorts maintain their own lobbying forces and make just enough effort to avoid stepping on each other's toes. Peaceful coexistence, I guess.

Mike Kaplan and I tried for several years to bring Vail Resorts back, including meetings with Rob Katz and Blaise Carrig, but to no avail. There's risk in not having a functioning forum whereby the industry can develop a common position on critical issues. Maybe the big one hasn't come up yet. When it does, things might change. Ironically, CSCUSA continues to do a great job representing the interests of its members, but that means recognizing that Vail Resorts is a big elephant in the room, and a competitive force that all need to appreciate and counter as appropriate. There's an argument that says Vail Resorts should have stayed in CSCUSA to influence its decision making rather than create an opposing force. Regardless, it was Rob Katz's decision. One he stands by, even if it's not understandable to the rest of us.

Some have offered the opinion that he just didn't believe in Melanie Mills, who was the clear consensus to succeed Rob Perlman. I don't buy that. Rob Katz has probably done more than any other resort chief to promote women in his organization. But in retrospect, it's still not understandable to me. Governor Hickenlooper was probably right: we just surprised him.

Most of the Vail Resorts executives we spoke to at the time expressed frustration at the departure and the way it had come down. But no one in that organization was going to change Katz's decision. The CEO reportedly does encourage vigorous debate and urges his executive-committee members to speak their minds. But in the Ski Country case, for whatever reason, he made the call. Life goes on. Vail Resorts is bigger than Colorado Ski Country.

IF YOU DON'T KNOW ROB KATZ, you might be envisioning some kind of ogre or demagogue. Quite the contrary. Socially, he's easy to converse with, approachable, and always curious. He hires good people and fires bad ones.

Blaise Carrig recently retired after some 15 years with Vail Resorts (starting as president of Heavenly, and winding up as president of the Mountain Division). I was fortunate to be at his retirement party in the summer of 2015, when Rob Katz made a brief but telling toast. He explained that Blaise had the special talent of being able to walk into Ski Patrol Headquarters, recognize inappropriate behavior on the part of a staff member, make the correction on the spot, but do so in a way that was respectful yet effective. It was a totally appropriate tribute to Blaise who, indeed, does have that skill set (and started his career as a patroller). But it was also interesting as a comment on what Rob Katz expected and would continue to expect from his leaders within the organization.

John Garnsey had been a longtime COO of Beaver Creek and then president of global mountain development from 2008 to 2014. When John stepped down from that role, he was kept on in an advisory capacity through the 2015 World Alpine Ski Championships, an event he had been closely associated with. This gave John a chance to transition in a positive, productive way.

Blaise became the senior mountain advisor for a period of two years following his official retirement. Katz is no doubt taking advantage of his availability for advice and direction as he continues to grow the organization. Knowing how to transition leadership and manage that change effectively is always a challenge. Katz does it well.

He also has the financial resources to lock in the best talent, and promotes from within whenever possible. Pat Campbell, who worked through the Vail Resorts ranks to become Keystone's president, took over the reins from Blaise in 2015 and now leads the Vail Resorts Mountain Division. She is the highest-ranking woman in the ski industry and in its history. Good for Vail.

As noted earlier, one of the conundrums that any ski-resort holding company faces is drawing the line on centralization versus decentralization. Public-company owners are totally focused on cost management through consolidation wherever possible. The risk in functional consolidation is that decisions move far enough way from the resort that they cease to support the brand. To date, Vail Resorts appears to have dodged this bullet. Beaver Creek maintains its distinct personality, ditto for Breckenridge and the other resorts. With rapid growth through acquisition and the distance now separating far-flung ski areas from the Broomfield HQ, the issue of centralized versus decentralized management will be more complex.

A huge advantage that the Vail Resorts group enjoys is the Epic Pass. It's more than a pass, it's a product that fully supports both the corporate brand and the individual resorts.

The first cheap season ski pass came out of Bogus Basin, Idaho, in the spring of 1998. Winter Park launched the "cheap pass" wars in Colorado shortly afterward, with a four-person product aimed at Front Range and other drive-in skiers that was dubbed the "Buddy Pass." Jerry Groswold, Winter Park's CEO at the time, waded into these waters reluctantly. The reality was that Winter Park was in danger of default and needed cash. Period. It sold an $800 season pass for four individuals ($200 each), an unheard-of bargain. Most of the remainder of the ski areas in Colorado immediately followed suit, but the passes targeted regional day—not destination—skiers.

Vail Resorts eventually took the affordable-pass strategy to another level by offering unlimited, unrestricted access to all its resorts, and aggressively marketing it to the world. Epic Pass marketing is truly a saturation strategy: website and digital targeting, TV, billboards, print, social media . . . everything leads with the Epic Pass. It screams "deal," and it reminds everyone that Vail Resorts is indeed Epic. While the company uses independent media to trumpet the message, it has built its own in-house custom-content focus and has the database that trumps all others.

From a business and bottom-line strategy, Epic is all about dramatically increasing volume and maintaining yield. We can use some rough, ballpark figures to illustrate. Back in an earlier era, the eight major resorts now under the Vail Resorts Epic Pass banner may have sold 50,000 total season passes to hardcore customers for an average price of $1,000 and total revenue of $50 million.

Now, with the conquer-the-world Epic Pass in its many interations, Vail Resorts is selling some 500,000 total passes annually. At an average price of $700, that would be $350 million.

More importantly, while the old hardcore season-pass holder skied 40-plus days a year, the average current Epic passholder's days are somewhere in the high single-digit range, maybe eight or nine.

For Vail Resorts, most of that lift-ticket revenue is in the bank before the first snow flies, a nice hedge in case it doesn't. The destination passholder, lured by cheap skiing, is booking trips and planning to spend much bigger money on ground transportation, lodging, meals, ski school, rentals/retail, and maybe even a condo, all controlled by Vail Resorts' vertically integrated resort operation.

Earlier, I mentioned its success with retail/rental and its SSV acquisition. In 2008, Vail Resorts entered the transportation business by purchasing Colorado Mountain Express (CME). I have no idea how the division performs from an EBITDA perspective, but it sure reinforces the Vail Resorts message. All vans seem to be wrapped with Epic messaging. Even driving to Denver in the summer, passing a CME van, the message is there. Vail is Epic. I imagine as well that if anyone in those vans was headed to a competing Front Range resort (a Copper or Winter Park), the driver would be making every effort to promote Vail Resorts for the next visit.

With Vail's daily ticket now closing in on $200 (and sister resorts close behind), the Epic Pass is a no-brainer for anyone planning a visit of four or five or more days to one of the Vail Resorts. Related products are available, such as the Epic Local Pass, where the price drops in proportion to added restrictions on usage. The ultimate beauty of Epic is its simplicity. It sells itself.

I don't think anyone ever thought that the "value pass" products would be offered to destination guests. There was always a desire to "fence" such products, so that they wouldn't cause diminished yield (per ticket) from the lucrative destination market. It think this is one of Rob Katz's greatest achievements. He watched the product grow in appeal, stuck with it, kept it simple, and never lost focus on the potential. Vail Resorts now presells 40 to 50 percent of its annual lift revenue.

Vail Resorts was not the first to provide a high-value season pass, but it took that strategy to the next level. In my time at Steamboat, which isn't close enough to the Front Range to attract day skiers, we couldn't drive the volume to compete at these price points. Unlike Vail's, our market was inelastic. Most of the other Intrawest resorts were also not geographically placed to enable us to make the leap together. So Steamboat falls into that second bucket of top destination resorts that aren't in close proximity to large metro areas, and still charge $1,000 to $2,000 for a season pass, a list that also includes resorts like Jackson Hole, Sun Valley, and Telluride.

Not that there aren't deals to be had. Intrawest, in conjunction with Powdr, does offer a multiresort value package that's highly competitive on the Front Range: the Rocky Mountain Super Pass Plus, which offered unlimited skiing at Winter Park, Copper, and Eldora, plus six days at Steamboat and two days at Crested Butte. It's a strong competitor in the Colorado market, but it's not a destination product by intent and structure. And it doesn't work for locals who want to ski more than six days at Steamboat. Other resorts have banded together to offer a destination-skier alternative to Epic, most notably the Mountain Collective, which offers two days of skiing at its member resorts. It is comprised primarily of independently owned resorts, including Alta and Snowbird; the four areas of Aspen Snowmass; Squaw Valley and Alpine Meadows; Jackson Hole; Mammoth; Sun Valley; Taos; Telluride; Stowe in the East; and Thredbo in Australia (and, for the 2016–17 season before it goes Epic, Whistler Blackcomb). Meanwhile, Intrawest, Powdr, Boyne Resorts, and other operators have combined to offer the M.A.X. (Multi-Alpine Experience) Pass, which offers five days at 32 resorts across North America. So many choices.

Even though all these other resorts have been bold and creative in providing alternatives, the Epic Pass still trumps them in volume and most metrics.

VAIL RESORTS ALSO EMPLOYS a guest database and a Customer Relations Management (CRM) program that dwarfs its competitors. As it acquires additional resorts, it "acquires" their guests and voilà . . . more Epic purchases. How happy are you in the Minneapolis, Detroit or Chicago metro areas to be able to ski at your local Vail Resorts–owned hill—Afton Alps, Mt. Brighton, and Wilmot

Mountain, respectively—and then enjoy free skiing at all of the company's sister resorts?

The flip side of Epic is dynamic pricing. I remember the "old days," where the sign shop produced the annual pricing signs in October or November. Pricing decisions were made when budgets were assembled, usually in the late spring. Prices never went up. Marketing departments "sold" by discounting against the published prices to compete and drive volume. Multiday pricing has continued to be fixed early in order to get group and tour sales pieces into the marketplace. However, within the last 10 years, resorts have begun to hold off on pricing shorter-term stays until the last minute. Most recently, following Vail Resorts' lead, one- and two-day tickets are priced daily by many of the larger resorts. Welcome to the world of dynamic pricing.

Vail Resorts still publishes its multiday prices for the season. Unless one pays no attention to the cost of the lift ticket, the best decision is usually to purchase the Epic pass if the plan is for five or more days of skiing. For the 2015–16 season, Vail's one-day ticket peaked at $159. If anyone complains, well: "Did you consider an Epic Pass?" End of discussion.

As a competitor for so many years, I always envied the Vail Resorts managers for their ready access to maintenance capital. I don't mean just replacing tired snowmaking pipe, rental fleets, and the like. But the big stuff: retiring old lifts and replacing them with state-of-the-art equipment before the older stuff fails or becomes unreliable. Having made many "sales" presentations to prospective ski-area buyers, I found the No. 1 question is always deferred maintenance: "What's deferred, and how much does it cost to catch up?"

That's because the numbers are often daunting and come right off the resort's valuation. For any major lift, replacement means upgrading to current technology. So replacing a 30-year-old fixed-grip quad at the end of its useful life requires an investment of $5 million to $8 million for a detachable, depending on length, vertical, etc. At least with the fixed-grip retirement, the resort gains an increment of capacity for its investment (the difference of the effective capacity of the fixed-grip lift versus the detachable). The ski-resort industry is now entering a time when the "first-generation" detachables, now pushing 30 years old, are ready for retirement. So many resorts are faced with the need to replace capacity with equivalent capacity. A painful "maintenance" investment, improving reliability and safety, but not generating additional revenue.

Vail Resorts, under Katz's leadership, has been notably aggressive in keeping its lift systems up-to-date. It's also part of the implied promise to consumers that when you visit a Vail Resorts–owned mountain, it is a world-class journey (or, as the company's ubiquitous tagline says, the "Experience of a Lifetime"). While there are exceptions in terms of resorts that have aggressively reinvested (Jackson Hole, Sun Valley, Snowbird, to name three), generally the competition lags far behind.

The same is true of other major infrastructure projects: snowmaking pipelines/compressors, on-moutain restaurants, etc. These facilities are generally in better shape at Vail Resorts–owned areas than elsewhere in the ski industry. Perhaps the most critical advantage that Vail Resorts' timely capital spending has provided: they don't face the need to divert future cash flows to maintenance capital. That cash can go to acquisitions or true growth capital investments at the resorts.

FOR SUMMER BUSINESS, Epic Discovery is bringing in counterseasonal income. Most resorts generate only 10 to 15 percent of their annual revenues in the summer. Vail Resorts will probably be at the high end of that number, thanks to its investments in summer attractons, and it will be able to look to the north for lessons learned at Whistler, which is the indisputable summer leader among the North America players for high-margin operations. The summer season in Colorado is even shorter than winter, so high margins are critical. Vail leverages some of these attractions during the winter as well, such as the mountain coaster.

While Vail has been the brunt of local jokes regarding its "Yellow Jacket" courtesy patrols, there is no question that they are a visible, on-mountain reminder of the company's commitment to and investment in skier safety.

In dealing with the negative business impacts of the Great Recession, I can remember consulting with Blaise and others in the industry regarding their strategies for managing costs. Blaise said his direction was clear in terms of total savings that were expected, but in no event were proposed changes to impact the frontline staff that delivers the guest experience. This reflects a sound direction from the top. It's also a reflection of the strength of the balance sheet and commitment to creating or maintaining value over the long term. Ironically, Vail Resorts had launched the destination portion of the Epic Pass program just before the recession hit in the fall of 2008. At high-end Vail in particular, local businesses had been concerned that the resort was now catering to the brown-bagging day skier. With destination visits hit hard by the economic downturn, those Epic-toting "day skiers" from the Front Range probably ended up salvaging Vail's season.

"KEEP IT SIMPLE, STUPID." I envision a small white board somewhere in Rob Katz's office with that message, although it's no doubt a digital affair given his tech bent. Whatever the format, it's a list of projects designed to simplify and focus the business. You can bet that all managers at Vail Resorts know exactly what's on that list.

Real-estate development is cyclical, erratic and complex compared to the operation of resorts, and it also sparks conflict in the host communities. I suspect that Rob Katz would be hard-pressed to do any vertical building. Find a development partner to take the risk (such as what Vail Resorts is planning with its "Ever Vail" project), and go forward only if it's a strategic investment that adds value to the larger resort enterprise and experience.

Real-estate sales are also best left to the professionals. Vail Resorts quietly participates as a partner in Slifer, Smith & Frampton, the big dog in Vail Valley real estate. I'm sure they share databases, but Vail Resorts is quietly in the background. In terms of total sales, the firm dominates the mountain-resort real-estate space.

BY NOW YOU MAY BE WONDERING if I'm on the Vail Resorts payroll. Not true. I just respect how Vail Resorts has evolved under the leadership of Rob Katz, and how quickly he has secured the current preeminent position the company enjoys. Remember, it was just nine years ago, in 2007, that Intrawest dwarfed Vail Resorts in skier visits and total revenues. While many of the big ski-area holding companies struggle to establish a valuation that exceeds that of the individual companies, for Vail Resorts there is no question. The whole *is* more valuable than the parts. The company is organized around that simple principle.

The credit goes to Rob Katz. That doesn't mean everything within the organization is hunky-dory. His managers bristle at the late-night calls from Rob complaining about the lack of gluten-free options at Two Elk ... or whatever.

Katz's energy seems to know no bounds. That doesn't mean that he's always focused on the most important things. While management grasps his strategy and leadership style, there does appear to be a disconnect farther down the ranks. Part of that disconnect just goes with the territory, being a large company with so many employees. But the business is, first and foremost, a service business. Employees need to be aligned with the mothership, supportive and enthusiastic about both their current situation and the future. Keeping a positive, service-oriented culture will be an increasing challenge as the company grows.

Complicating the service challenge is the impact of the Epic Pass on weekends and holidays at Vail, and to a certain extent its sister resorts. Nothing generates a comparable level of conversation or criticism. If Vail is indeed all about the ski experience, and has made the capital investments to ensure that experience, why does it allow its prize property to be literally overrun?

When *SKI* Magazine launched its Reader Resort Rankings in the mid-1980s, Vail became the perennial No. 1, collecting the top spot in 13 of the first 17 seasons. In the past decade, and despite a village rennaissance and aggressive, strategic improvements on the mountain, it has been pushed down in the rankings, with crowds and character (and the cost of parking) among the major complaints.

If you are a high-end destination guest, spending more than $20,000 for your family's weeklong vacation, waiting a half-hour in liftlines doesn't cut it. For most weekends and holidays, Vail is an urban experience. Ditto for their other destination properties.... Beaver Creek being least impacted, given its access and parking issues. (Which might be about to change, with Vail Resorts' unpopular decision to charge $10 for parking in the previously free day-skier lots at the base of the resort for the 2016–17 season).

But so far, the numbers don't lie. People grumble, but line up to repurchase their next Epic Pass. The future? I have to believe that the price is going up at the premier properties, and usage restrictions will be added to help even out demand, eventually lessening the negative impact on Vail Mountain. Time will tell.

One area where the company could face pitfalls is in the political arena. Vail Resorts was very visible in its financial support of the 2008 Democratic National Convention in Denver, donating $500,000 to also weave an environmental theme into the affair. I watched the damage that picking political sides did to S-K-I under Pres Smith. Since those days, my personal political philosophy is something that I very consciously separate from the business. Especially in the ski business, we get into enough fights without picking them. So standing back and ensuring good political equilibrium regardless of which party is in power seems to be the best strategy. Vail Resorts has made a political choice as a company and could pay a price if/when the tide turns, as it always does.

SO WHERE IS VAIL RESORTS HEADED NEXT? In the first draft of this manuscript, I predicted the company would make a game-changing play for that other North American resort juggernaut, Whistler Blackcomb. Before we went to press, it happened. With the accouncement in August 2016 of the $1 billion deal, the Vail Resorts family now includes the three most popular resorts in North America: Whistler Blackcomb, Vail, and Breckenridge. Katz has now combined the strongest American and Canadian companies in the business, and they have complementary customer bases.

Vail Resorts will also certainly find a way to enter the Northeastern market, regardless of the weather vagaries and the challenges of providing the "Experience of a Lifetime" under those conditions. A property such as Killington would be a very desirable acquisition. Killington is the largest area in the East, with arguably the largest customer base. Selling Epic, with unlimited Killington skiing and access to the Western properties . . . what a value proposition. Killington still dominates in the New York and New Jersey markets. A smaller property in New Hampshire or Maine would place the Boston market in the Vail Resorts fold. Opinion only, but I think it's just a matter of time.

One resort in the Washington, D.C., market would open up the Southeast. Another Canadian foray could include Mont-Sainte-Anne in Quebec, opening doors in the eastern Canadian market, which boasts a large skier and rider base. While Vail is already a big player in California, it must be tempting to Rob Katz to think of acquiring Mammoth and its two Southern California resorts. Rumors have ownership looking to sell. Antitrust considerations might force Vail Resorts to dispose of some other California asset(s), but what another game changer this would be.

Isn't it fun to speculate! If you've hung with me this far, I think you will agree that Vail Resorts is not done. But there will be fewer easy targets (we'll not see a Park City deal again), and the price is going up, as it did with Whistler.

CHAPTER 18

Future Challenges:

Who Will Lead?

So how will Vail Resorts' growth on one hand and the relative détente within the rest of the industry affect the skier experience? Well, there's plenty of competition, so values should continue to abound . . . assuming the consumer makes an up-front investment in a pass product.

The business of operating ski resorts is a profitable one. That said, resorts have been very cautious about capital investments given the recent recession. The time is coming when lift replacements can no longer be postponed, so I believe the next few years will see a big jump in capital spending. New facilities and expansions are a way to compete and differentiate your product. Jackson Hole has been notably successful in leveraging its improvements, despite being an independent. We may even see some proposed terrain expansions. It used to be that "if you build it they will come." Not true on the "building" side for many years. But some recent resort expansions suggest that the old maxim needs dusting off.

Loon Mountain is experiencing a significant renaissance thanks to its South Mountain expansion. Okemo leveraged its late-1990s Jackson Gore expansion to move into second place in terms of total New England skier visits (behind only Killington). It will be interesting to observe how a Squaw/Alpine

Interconnect moves the attendance figures. While I don't see a huge growth spurt ahead for U.S. resorts, I do think we will see targeted expansions that will, in turn, force competitive responses. Skiers and riders should benefit.

AND THAT PROVIDES A SEGUE to the role of the U.S. Forest Service. This once-proud group of conservationist professionals has been decimated by spending cuts at the national level. The USFS was led by timber and forest management professionals until the National Environmental Policy Act (NEPA) effectively shut down commercial logging in our national forests. The professionals that ran the agency during the formative years of the U.S. ski industry have all retired or moved on, and they are sorely missed. There is very little skiing history now embedded in the agency. Decisions are more "political," reflecting the views of the current occupant of the White House. Further complicating the situation, the annual budgets that once supported recreation are now being diverted to support firefighting, a trend that will not change, given the impacts of climate change. The combination of lost talent and reduced budgets has created a painfully slow permit-approval process. Resorts are shouldering more and more of the costs relative to permit acquisition. Meanwhile, the USFS sits back and says, "Sorry, we just don't have the resources."

Ski areas that operate on national forest land pay millions annually in fees; the 22 Colorado resorts operating on USFS land contributed a record $23 million for the 2014–15 season alone. Those dollars go straight to the U.S. Treasury, but a portion should be returned to the local forests and the communities that have helped create that income. Will it happen? Ron Wyden, a U.S. senator from Oregon, has proposed such legislation. It's so logical, it might have a chance, even in this day and age of political gridlock.

The "brain drain" we've noticed within the USFS is happening in the ski industry as well. NSAA's Michael Berry calls this one of the greatest challenges currently facing the ski industry. He likes to remind aging operators like myself that when we were moving into management some 40 years ago, there were maybe 40 top jobs and twice as many capable managers competing for those spots. Resorts were focused on talent development, and because it was a period of dramatic growth, there were many opportunities for those who stepped away from traditional careers to try skiing. Some companies, like Killington, actually invested in management training (remember that Les Otten went through the Killington program).

I remember an interview that David Rowan of *SAM* did with Pres Smith back in the 1970s. When he asked Pres his philosophy of management, the answer went something like this: "I look at my management team like horses in a horse race. I always keep an extra one in the starting gate in case another one stumbles."

Those were the days. Ski-area managers learned how to do more with less in the interim, and bench strength went by the wayside. Put simply, there is a dearth of top-level talent at a time when the Boomers are retiring. Vail Resorts, given its size, has been able to focus resources on staff development and to promote from within to meet the challenges of new acquisitions. Other resorts are not so fortunate.

MICHAEL BERRY HAS LED THE NSAA for some 25 years. He has played a key role in the sharing of best practices across the country. Bottom line: a vastly more consumer-friendly and margin-friendly operating model. NSAA is strong financially and enjoys an excellent reputation as the spokesperson for U.S. ski-resort operators. And Berry has driven broad acceptance of the "Model for Growth." The U.S. industry has never enjoyed healthier balance sheets. The future remains bright, even in the context of global warming.

Michael is retiring in the next few years. Finding an individual to carry on his excellent work will be a challenge, for the same reasons noted above. The talent pool is shallow. But finding the right person is so very important, because a high-performing NSAA is now critical to the success of the ski industry.

Snowsports Industries America (SIA) saw the recent retirement of 39-year veteran David Ingemie. The jury is out on the new leadership, the nonprofit's severe reduction of its staff, and its move from McLean, Virginia, to Park City. SIA is a shadow of its former self, as the trade show has diminished in size. Retailing is simply a changed world, and the ski-shop business is not isolated from larger, disruptive trends. Back in the late 1980s, SIA was the big dog in the ski business. You'll remember the unfortunate marriage with NSAA that ended in divorce. Ironically, today it is NSAA that's the economic engine of U.S. skiing. Along with the competitively focused U.S. Ski and Snowboard Team, the other associations critical to the success of U.S. skiing are the PSIA (Professional Ski Instructors of America) and the NSP (National Ski Patrol). Both of the latter have had recent changes in leadership.

I think the time has come where NSAA needs to provide a new level of support to PSIA and NSP and should bring them inside the tent. All parties will be better served if we can move to a higher level of collaboration. What I envision is an annual summit of the key players: NSAA, SIA, PSIA, NSP and the U.S. Ski Team. They gather at the same table and talk to the big issues that each organization faces . . . and look for common solutions and strategies. Perhaps the time has come. At a minimum, these groups all need to be led by individuals who can embrace the entire picture and not just their corner of it.

CHAPTER 19

A Better Resort Model:

Stakeholder Buy-In

So after all these pages of stories and opinions, what's the best model of ownership for the ski area of the future? It's a somewhat academic question, given that we have a variety of high-functioning models already in place. But I'd like to propose a better way, a route that could support the existing ownership models.

My proposal does not apply to smaller, urban facilities that operate in larger communities, where they are one of several recreation providers. These are not "ski towns." Nor would it apply to the handful of "private-club type" resorts that are appearing.

The great majority of skier visits in the U.S. come from resorts that are in or near ski towns, or mountain towns. These are regional or national ski destinations. The town might have existed before the resort (an Aspen, Stowe, or Park City) or grew up alongside it (Vail, Waterville Valley). In either case, they have evolved into the modern ski towns we know and love.

These are appealing places to live. An active, outdoor lifestyle is cherished, and while there's typically a huge variety of activities, the ski area remains the focal point. Some residents may have stopped skiing due to age or injury, but the ski area was the reason they first came to town. As the local saying goes in mountain towns across the country, "I came for the winter but stayed for the summer." For many, the ski area was their first job, the place where they first met their spouse, where the kids learned to ski, where their memories abound. The emotional connection is hugely powerful but generally underappreciated.

What happens at the ski area has an outsized impact on the "ski town." Remember the trauma ASC caused in Steamboat? The cumulative gaffes of Les Otten created a perception that he was going to damage the ski-area's image and eventually the community itself. And the community responded.

Wouldn't it be better if everyone had some skin in the game with the ability to influence the strategic direction of the resort? Not for free. I'm talking investing . . . putting some money at risk in exchange for a seat at the table.

This is not a Bernie Sanders version of how the ski business should operate. Success in a capitalist system derives from equity investors willing to take risks, and those investors need considerable control over what happens to the investment. That doesn't mean that partners can't be brought in. The first should be the community. A town like Steamboat Springs should have an investment in the resort. Maybe 5 or 10 percent of the equity value. Then, do you think the regulatory process might be more responsive? Sitting on the "board," the city could look at how its capital plans support and are supported by the larger investments at the mountain. If capital was needed for important projects, the city could participate—or not. If they declined, then their ownership percentage would be proportionately diminished.

A percentage of ownership should be made available to local businesses, which are so impacted by the performance of the ski area. If you want a say, invest.

The state (if the land is so owned) or the federal government (if USFS land-based) should, in an ideal world, also have a piece of the pie. Polyannish? Perhaps. But you can't say that the current model is highly efficient. What better way to ensure collaboration than to invite the landowner to the table: "And be sure to bring a check."

Finally, since the success or failure of the ski area is so closely tied to the quality of life in mountain towns, locals should have the chance to "buy in," to share the rewards of success but share the pain when times are tough.

If an additional 15 percent of new equity were invested (at market rates) alongside the original owners *and* the new capital was put to productive use, the result should be a stronger company and no dilution. It's just a new form of governance, probably a bit clumsy for a few years, since the stakeholders are going to have to master a new way of decision making. Original ownership would still have control, but the new stakeholders would bring a fresh perspective to the table, emphasizing issues such as a cooperative approach to providing affordable employee housing.

This idea should have legs for several reasons. The most important is the potential for alignment and collaboration beyond the status quo. A secondary benefit would be that the broader community, now "investors," could focus on service in a more coordinated way. If a Steamboat guest has a wonderful experience at the mountain but a bad experience with the local taxi service, that affects the whole vacation. An entire community focused on the quality and consistency of service—and vice versa, having all of the stakeholders focusing on the local quality-of-life issues needed to support it—would raise the bar in an incredible way. And it would be a great place to live.

THE BUSINESS OF SKIING has changed dramatically over the past 44 years. Visionaries like Pres Smith and Dave McCoy had the willpower and tenacity to create world-class ski areas from literally raw land ... and build entire communities in the process. Both of their creations, Killington and Mammoth, are now part of larger holding companies. Has something been lost in that transition? Absolutely. Does each resort still have a distinctive appeal that reflects the original visions of those men? Yes.

It's possible that a generation from now, their touch will be less visible— and the personalities less remembered. But it will still exist in the design, trail names, architecture, and all those little touches that combine to define each resort's brand.

Watching the sport grow over four-plus decades, and having the experience of working with so many unique, creative personalitites, has been simply wonderful. Skiing deserves bigger-than-life leaders, and we have been fortunate to have them. It would seem inevitable that increased corporate influence will temper the creativity that, to date, has defined the sport. But maybe not. The people I have had the pleasure of working with day in and day out are still just big kids on a powder day. I think that will save us.

I hope that you've enjoyed sharing my experiences and thoughts on the ski business. I have been fortunate to work with many wonderful characters, some of whom you've met in these pages. I couldn't have made this trip without them.

APPENDIX

The below circa-1970 copy was written by Killington Marketing Director Foster T. Chandler. It appeared in magazine advertisements in titles ranging from *TIME* to *The New Yorker*, and was also published in dougle-page spreads in the major daily newspapers.

A Little Bit of Purple Prose About Learning to Ski

A lot of people will give you this thing about the courage of the first man who ate an oyster.

We would respectfully suggest that he had nothing on the first guy who strapped himself to a pair of oak staves and headed for the nearest mountain.

Whoever he was, wherever he roamed, anyone who's learned that same old way will tell you that if the first skier had nothing else, he had guts.

In fact, until quite recently, guts was the most important single ingredient in learning to ski.

A dramatic development.

Recently, within the last 9 years, a new method of ski instruction has been developed and perfected at Killington.

It is called the Accelerated Ski Method™ (formerly known as GLM). If you have even a shred of desire, plus enough coordination to have picked up this magazine, you can learn to ski the Accelerated way.

Guts is no longer the pivotal requirement.

A great idea.

Instead of strapping you into a pair of 6 or 7 foot skis and sending you onto the hill, the Accelerated Ski Method works you up to full-size gradually. Your first lesson is on 39-inch instruction skis. If you can walk you can get around on these.

Once you've mastered the rhythm and gained confidence you move up to 60-inch, mid-length, training skis. When you have them conquered, you move on to skis which are standard for your height and weight.

Instead of struggling for days with "herringbones" and "sidestepping," you will be skiing, unassisted, in your very first hour. You will amaze yourself.

Some fabulous plans.

Learning to ski is *not* impossible. It's also not as expensive as everyone's told you.

At Killington, we've put together amazingly inexpensive learn-to-ski vacations, which include everything but your "longjohns." The very finest skis, mounted with the most advanced release bindings. Top quality buckle boots and poles. Hundreds of dollars worth of equipment better than most beginners buy for themselves.

All this, plus lifts, plus lessons costs $40 for a 2-day introductory weekend. For 5 days midweek, we throw in a few extras and charge $70.

Don't expect any miracles with the weekend plan unless you can put together three or four weekends back to back. But, if by the end of a 5-day midweek vacation, you're not a proficient skier, then you are very probably unteachable.

Some terrific skiing.

Once you learn, you'll find that Killington won't bore you. There are four mountains to ski. Among the more than four dozen trails, you'll find the longest one east of the Rocky Mountains.

Of our eleven lifts, one, the new Killington gondola, is the longest ski lift in the world! And, as you might expect, there are a great many places to rest your bones and pick up your spirits when the lifts have closed.

(The ad closed with a call to write Foster for more information and this prediction: "If we know old Foster, he'll absolutely bombard you with brochures, pamphlets, and all that.")

North American Ski Resort Ownership*
(as of September 1, 2016)

United States

Alpine Valley Holding Co.
Alpine Valley, Michigan
Alpine Valley Resort, Wisconsin
Bittersweet Resort, Michigan
Devil's Head Resort, Wisconsin
Mt. Holly Ski Area, Michigan
Pine Knob Ski Area, Michigan

Aspen Skiing Company
Aspen Highlands, Colorado
Aspen Mountain, Colorado
Buttermilk, Colorado
Snowmass Ski and Snowboard Resort,
    Colorado

Boyne USA, Inc.
Big Sky Resort, Montana
*Brighton Resort, Utah
Boyne Highlands Resort, Michigan
Boyne Mountain Resort, Michigan
Crystal Mountain Resort, Washington
*Cypress Mountain, British Columbia
*Loon Mountain, New Hampshire
*Sugarloaf, Maine
*The Summit at Snoqualmie, Washington
*Sunday River, Maine

*Resorts are owned by CNL Lifestyle
Properties and operated under long-term
agreement by Boyne USA.

Intrawest
Blue Mountain, Ontario
Snowshoe, West Virginia
Steamboat Ski & Resort Corporation,
    Colorado
Stratton, Vermont
Tremblant, Quebec
*Winter Park Resort, Colorado

Note: Winter Park is owned by the City and
County of Denver and operated by Intrawest.
Intrawest also owns a 15 percent interest in
Mammoth, California.

KSL Capital Partners
Alpine Meadows, California
Squaw Valley, California

Mammoth Mountain Ski Area LLC
Bear Mountain Resort, California
June Mountain, California
Mammoth, California
Snow Summit, California

Peak Resorts, Inc.
Alpine Valley, Ohio
Attitash, New Hampshire
Big Boulder Ski Area, Pennsylvania
Boston Mills/Brandywine, Ohio
Crotched Mt., New Hampshire
Hidden Valley, Missouri
Hunter Mountain, New York
Jack Frost, Pennsylvania
*Mad River Mountain, Ohio
Mount Snow, Vermont
Paoli Peaks, Indiana
Snow Creek, Missouri
Wildcat Mountain, New Hampshire

*Resort is is owned by EPR Properties and
    operated under a long-term agreement by
    Peak Resorts, Inc.

Powdr Corp.
Boreal Mountain Resort, California
Copper Mountain, Colorado
Eldora Mountain Resort, Colorado
Gorgoza Tubing Park, Utah
Killington, Vermont
Lee Canyon, Nevada
Mt. Bachelor, Oregon
Pico Mountain, Vermont
Soda Springs Mountain Resort, California

Sinclair Oil Corporation
Snowbasin, Utah
Sun Valley, Idaho

Snow Time, Inc.
Liberty Mountain Resort, Pennsylvania
Roundtop Mountain Resort, Pennsylvania
Whitetail Resort, Pennsylvania

State of New York
Belleayre Mountain (Olympic Regional
    Development Authority)
Gore Mountain (Olympic Regional
    Development Authority)
Whiteface (Olympic Regional
    Development Authority)

Triple Peaks LLC
*Crested Butte Mountain Resort,
    Colorado
**Mount Sunapee, New Hampshire
*Okemo Mountain Resort, Vermont
**Resorts are owned by CNL Lifestyle
    Properties and operated under long-term
    agreement by Triple Peaks LLC.
**Resort is owned by State of New Hampshire.
    CNL Lifestyle Properties has lease rights and
    it is operated under long-term agreement by
    Triple Peaks, LLC.

Vail Resorts, Inc.
Afton Alps, Minnesota
Beaver Creek Resort, Colorado
Breckenridge Resort, Colorado
Heavenly, California/Nevada
Keystone Resort, Colorado
Kirkwood Mountain Resort, California
Mt. Brighton, Michigan
*Northstar California, California
Park City Mountain, Utah
Perisher, Australia
Vail Mountain, Colorado
Whistler Blackcomb, British Columbia
Wilmot Mountain, Wisconsin
*Resort is owned by CNL Lifestyle Properties
    and operated under a long-term agreement
    by Vail Resorts, Inc.

Canada

Mont Saint-Sauveur International Inc.
Edelweiss, Ottawa
Mont Avila, Quebec
Ski Mont Gabriel, Quebec
Mont Olympia, Quebec
Mont Saint-Sauveur, Quebec
Ski Morin Heights, Quebec

Resorts of the Canadian Rockies, Inc.
Fernie Alpine Resort, British Columbia
Kicking Horse Mountain Resort, British
    Columbia
Kimberley Alpine Resort, British
    Columbia
Mont-Sainte-Anne, Quebec
Nakiska Ski Area, Alberta
Stoneham Mountain Resort, Quebec
Note: CNL Lifestyle Corp. also owns
Mountain High Resort, California (operated
under long-term agreement by Mountain High
Associates), Sierra-at-Tahoe, California
(operated under long-term agreement by Booth
Creek Ski Holdings Inc.), Stevens Pass,
Washington (operated under long-term
agreeement by Stevens Pass Mountain Resort,
LLC), and Jiminy Peak Mountain Resort,
Massachusetts and Cranmore Mountain
Resort, New Hampshire (both operated under
long-term agreement by Jiminy Peak Mountain
Resort, LLC).

*Source: National Ski Areas Association,
    Lakewood, Colorado

INDEX